Deuteronomy

Westminster Bible Companion

Series Editors

Patrick D. Miller
David L. Bartlett

Deuteronomy

THOMAS W. MANN

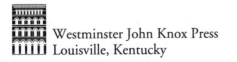

Westminster John Knox Press
Louisville, Kentucky

Book design by Publishers' WorkGroup
Cover design by Drew Stevens

First edition
Published by Westminster John Knox Press
Louisville, Kentucky

This book is printed on acid-free paper that meets the American National Standards Institute Z39.48 standard. ∞

PRINTED IN THE UNITED STATES OF AMERICA

95 96 97 98 99 00 01 02 03 04 — 10 9 8 7 6 5 4 3 2 1

Library of Congress Cataloging-in-Publication Data

Mann, Thomas W. (Thomas Wingate), 1944–
     Deuteronomy / Thomas W. Mann — 1st ed.
          p.   cm. — (Westminster Bible companion)
     ISBN 0-664-25266-4 (alk. paper)
     1. Bible. O.T. Deuteronomy—Commentaries.   I. Title.
II. Series.
BS1275.3.M36   1995
222'.15077—dc20   95-34834

In memory of Professor Bernard Boyd
who introduced me to the critical enjoyment of scripture
and in gratitude to all my other teachers

Contents

Series Foreword

This series of study guides to the Bible is offered to the church and more specifically to the laity. In daily devotions, in church school classes, and in listening to the preached word, individual Christians turn to the Bible for a sustaining word, a challenging word, and a sense of direction. The word that scripture brings may be highly personal as one deals with the demands and surprises, the joys and sorrows, of daily life. It also may have broader dimensions as people wrestle with moral and theological issues that involve us all. In every congregation and denomination, controversies arise that send ministry and laity alike back to the Word of God to find direction for dealing with difficult matters that confront us.

A significant number of lay women and men in the church also find themselves called to the service of teaching. Most of the time they will be teaching the Bible. In many churches, the primary sustained attention to the Bible and the discovery of its riches for our lives have come from the ongoing teaching of the Bible by persons who have not engaged in formal theological education. They have been willing, and often eager, to study the Bible in order to help others drink from its living water.

This volume is part of a series of books, the Westminster Bible Companion, intended to help the laity of the church read the Bible more clearly and intelligently. Whether such reading is for personal direction or for the teaching of others, the reader cannot avoid the difficulties of trying to understand these words from long ago. The scriptures are clear and clearly available to everyone as they call us to faith in the God who is revealed in Jesus Christ and as they offer to every human being the word of salvation. No companion volumes are necessary in order to hear such words truly. Yet every reader of scripture who pauses to ponder and think further about any text has questions that are not immediately answerable simply by reading the text of scripture. Such questions may be about historical and geographical details or about words that are obscure or so loaded with meaning that one cannot tell at a glance what is at stake. They may be about the fundamental meaning of a passage or about what connection a particular text might have to our contemporary world. Or a teacher preparing for a church school class may simply want to know: What should I say about this biblical passage when I have to teach it next Sunday? It is our hope that these volumes, written by teachers and pastors with long experience studying and teaching the Bible in the church, will help members of the church who want and need to study the Bible with their questions.

The New Revised Standard Version of the Bible is the basis for the interpretive comments that each author provides. The NRSV text is presented at the beginning of the discussion so that the reader may have at hand in a single volume both the scripture passage and the exposition of its meaning. In some instances, where inclusion of the entire passage is not necessary for understanding either the text or the interpreter's discussion, the presentation of the NRSV text may be abbreviated. Usually, the whole of the biblical text is given.

We hope this series will serve the community of faith, opening the Word of God to all the people, so that they may be sustained and guided by it.

Introduction

In the year 1630 the good ship *Arbella* approached the shores of New England and the Massachusetts Bay Colony with a group of pilgrims on board. Their leader, John Winthrop, realizing both the excitement and the apprehension of the moment, preached a sermon that would become a hallmark of the history of religion in America—"A Modell of Christian Charity." Winthrop reminded his shipmates that they had "entered into Covenant" with God, and that their future in "the good land whither wee are goeing" would depend on obedience to the "Articles" of the covenant. He concluded his sermon with a stirring quotation from the book of Deuteronomy: "Therefore lett us choose life, that wee, and our Seede, may live; by obeyeing his voyce, and cleaveing to him, for hee is our life, and our prosperity" (30:19–20).

On virtually every Sunday morning somewhere in *contemporary* America, a group of twentieth-century "pilgrims" can be found singing the old gospel hymn "On Jordan's Stormy Banks": "On Jordan's stormy banks I stand, and cast a wishful eye, to Canaan's fair and happy land, where my possessions lie." If you were to ask the singers what they mean by "Canaan," they would probably describe not a geographical but a spiritual reality; indeed, the hymn concludes with words that clearly understand Canaan as a symbol for heaven.

These two situations, spanning over three hundred years, illustrate the range of interpretive possibilities presented by the book of Deuteronomy. On the one hand, Winthrop was neither the first nor the last to apply the biblical language of a promised land and a chosen people to the "New World" of (North) America, and to find in the covenant theology of Deuteronomy a "modell" for a political community here on earth that sees God as ruler. On the other hand, the hymn singers attest to a more symbolic application of the language in which "Jordan's stormy banks" refer to the individual's spiritual condition, and the Promised Land becomes an otherworldly reality beyond this life. Of course, these two situations do not exhaust the interpretive possibilities, nor are they mutually exclusive. The "spirituals" of black slaves, for example, reveal a profound combination of the political and the spiritual understandings. "Canaan" could refer to an inner sense of freedom but also to the Underground Railroad and Canada.

Contemporary readers of Deuteronomy will do well to keep in mind the range of understanding that spans the personal and the political. They will also benefit from recognizing, along with Winthrop and our modern hymn singers, that the dramatic situation of Deuteronomy—poised between past and future, on the verge of the promised land—is fraught with meaning on many different levels. Indeed, the authors of the book composed it precisely in this way so that it would speak to each subsequent generation. Far from being a relic of ancient history, Deuteronomy is an urgent message addressed to the present, both to the present of the authors and to our own.

Deuteronomy gets its name from the Greek word *deuteronomion*, which means "second law," a mistranslation of the Hebrew phrase in Deuteronomy 17:18 that means "a copy of this law." The translators understood the book to be an addition to the law previously given at Sinai (Exod. 19—23). While in some respects this is true (particularly from a critical perspective), it is also misleading. Much of the book is more accurately described as a *completion* of a process that began at Sinai (called Horeb in Deuteronomy). The word for "copy" could also be translated "repetition." In one sense, this is the primary concern of the authors of the book: the repetition of Moses' words throughout the generations. Indeed, according to Jewish tradition the title of the book is its opening phrase, "these are the words." These are the words that need to be repeated by and for each member of the community, from the king to the ordinary citizen. Repetition means much more than copying (17:18; 27:3) or reciting the words out loud (31:9–13). It includes everything from daily conversations with children about these words (6:4–7) to the economic policies of the society built on them (Deut. 15).

We talk about the "three Rs" as the basics of education today. Deuteronomy has "four Rs": retelling, ratification, reinterpretation, and response.

RETELLING THE STORY

Deuteronomy is a *retelling* of stories from Israel's past. Especially in the first half of the book (chaps. 1—11), the authors repeat stories of particular importance for Israel's identity, stories already recorded in the books of Exodus and Numbers. So Moses reminds his audience of the shameful failure to take the land of Canaan, which led to the period of wandering in the wilderness (Deut. 1:19–46), then jumps to the more recent journeys through East Jordan (chaps. 2—3), turns back to the events at Horeb (that is, Sinai, receiving the Ten Commandments; chaps. 4—5), and then to the incident at Massah (6:16). In chapter 8 Moses returns to the story of the manna in the wilderness, and in chapters 9—10 he again refers to the time at Sinai/Horeb and the making of the golden calf.

Remembering these stories is Israel's way of knowing who they are and how they are to live. Forgetting these stories will lead to disaster. "Take care that you do not forget" (8:11) is an exhortation that pervades the entire book. Communal amnesia is a terminal illness. When a people forgets its past, it is unable to understand its present or rightly to enter its future. As we shall see, memory (like repetition) means far more than mere recall: it means living in a particular way that is in accord with one's past. For Deuteronomy, such living is "righteousness" (6:20–25); it is living in right relation to one's personal and community history and, above all, to the God who is known through that history. Sometimes, in order to instill a particular form of behavior, parents will say to their children, "that's not the way you were brought up." In a sense, and sometimes literally (as in 8:14), that is what Moses is doing when he retells stories from Israel's past—he is urging the people to live in accordance with what they remember.

RATIFYING THE COVENANT

Just as the retelling of stories is concentrated in chapters 1—11, so the giving of specific laws is concentrated in chapters 12—26. If "second law" is not the most appropriate title for the book, it does suggest rightly that much of the book has to do with law and, more broadly, with legal process.

As the conclusion of the formal law code suggests (26:16–19), the book reflects a process of legal *ratification*. The people are confirming a contract between themselves and Yahweh, their God, by agreeing to the terms of the contract as previously stated. The terms include not only what Moses has just declared to them but also the stipulations or laws given earlier at Sinai, as related in the book of Exodus. Much of the rest of Deuteronomy concerns the details of this ratification: Chapters 27—28 list sanctions to reward obedience to the covenant conditions (blessings) and to punish breach of covenant (curses); 31:9–13 discusses the deposit of the contract document and provisions for periodic public reading.

Much of the overall shape of the book of Deuteronomy reflects this concern for covenant ratification. In fact, the authors have adapted a model from the political language of their world and applied it to the relationship between Israel and God. A relatively small and militarily weak state would enter into a treaty with a larger and more powerful state, thereby gaining its protection, even if also having to pay for it by way of tribute. In such situations, the king of the powerful state (or "Great King") was the suzerain; the king of the lesser state was the vassal. A treaty was often enacted as a result of former acts of goodwill by the Great King (for example, rescue from enemies) and out of the gratitude of the vassal. Ratification of the treaty would frequently entail absolute allegiance to the Great King, prohibiting formal relationships with other "lords." The vassal's rewards for obeying the treaty would include continued sovereignty over one's territory, protection from enemies, and perhaps trade benefits. Punishments for breach of treaty were often severe: military destruction and exile.

Much of the content of Deuteronomy reflects the elements of such political treaties, as does much of the structure of the book: It moves from historical prologue, that is, the Great King's acts of benevolence (Deut. 1—11) to detailed conditions (chaps. 12—26) to rewards and punishments (chaps. 27—29). Accordingly, the Lord is understood as Israel's Great King, and Israel is the Lord's vassal. The result is a political system rooted in a covenant theology, and the bedrock of the biblical notion of the "kingdom [or 'realm'] of God."

It would be difficult to exaggerate the significance of this political model to biblical theology, including the New Testament, as well as to subsequent church and secular history. One thinks immediately of the central sacrament of the church, the "new covenant" celebrated in Holy Communion, or the Lord's Supper, and of a covenant tradition in political theory and practice that we glimpsed above in John Winthrop.

REINTERPRETING TRADITION

Deuteronomy thus represents a ratification of the treaty between God and Israel. At the same time, it also presents a *reinterpretation* of what that treaty means, not only for the Israel of Moses' time but for the Israel of all generations. The retelling of stories and laws is not simply wooden. The stories and laws are often adapted to fit new situations in the life of Israel. For example, Moses must die outside the promised land because of the people's sin, not his own, thus emphasizing that the community's breach of covenant may even overwhelm the relative good of individual leaders (3:23–27; note also the conflicting tradition retained in 32:48–52, reflecting Num. 20:12).

Laws that were known earlier in Exodus appear in Deuteronomy in a different way. For example, the law on freeing slaves is extended to cover women as well as men (Deut. 15:12–18), thus making justice more inclusive (contrast Exod. 21:7). In the regulations of Passover, the festival is prohibited from local celebrations and reserved for one location, conforming to one of the major reforms championed by the book—the centralization of all worship in one sanctuary (Deut. 16:5–6; contrast the household celebration in Exod. 12:1–13).

The reinterpretation of stories and laws lies at the heart of the meaning of Deuteronomy. The book is a record of reevaluations of Israel's central traditions in the light of changing situations, stretching over a period of at least several hundred years. Like most of the biblical books, Deuteronomy is not a "book" in the modern sense. It was not written by a single individual at a single time, much less by Moses. While some traditions described in it may well go back to Moses and his time, much of the book comes from later times, after the people had settled in the land. Indeed, many events that occurred after the time of Moses appear to be reflected: the institution of a monarchy, the construction of a temple, the rise of a commercial economy, conflicts with Canaanite culture and religion, the activity of prophets, civil war—and, by no means least, the threat of exile imposed by powerful empires in Assyria and Babylonia.

Some scholars suggest that we think of an ongoing Deuteronomic "school" as the source of what is now Deuteronomy. This is why I speak of "the authors" rather than a single author, although I may at times refer to "the Deuteronomist" as a collective entity. The earliest representatives of this school apparently took such traditions as the Ten Commandments (the Decalogue) and related texts (for example, Exod. 23:13–33 and 34:10–26) and used them as the basis for reforms within Israelite theology, law, and worship. The earliest efforts at reform may have occurred in the north (the northern kingdom of Israel, as distinct politically from Judah in the south) and show connections with the prophetic movement (for instance, Elijah in the ninth century, Hosea in the eighth).

Two of the major stages in the development of Deuteronomy occurred in conjunction with two monarchs who carried out reforms. Ruling in

Judah soon after the fall of Israel to the Assyrians in 721 B.C.E. ("Before Common Era"—formerly designated "B.C."). Hezekiah and his court scholars instituted numerous religious reforms (2 Kings 18:1–8). It is likely that a major portion of Deuteronomy was produced during this time (Deut. 4—28). A subsequent edition of the book probably appeared under the young king Josiah (640–609 B.C.E.), adding the framework to the book (Deut. 1—3, 29—34) and placing Deuteronomy itself at the beginning of a larger historical work called the Deuteronomistic History, which includes the books of Joshua through 2 Kings (without Ruth).

Josiah was the champion of the Deuteronomic school, the model king "according to all the law of Moses" (2 Kings 23:25; compare Deut. 34: 10–12). During his reign "the book of the law" was found in the temple; it was probably the long-neglected work produced under Hezekiah. Josiah reaffirmed the covenant with the Lord and proceeded to implement systematic reforms. Yet the young king met a tragic death in battle with the Egyptians, and the rest of the history of the Judean monarchy was a rapid decline into ruin. Within twenty-five years, Jerusalem was destroyed by the Babylonians, the temple was burned, the current king was blinded and hauled off in chains in Babylon, and the nation of Judah was no more. What was left of Israel existed only in exile.

Some of the latest additions to Deuteronomy probably come from this catastrophic period when Israel was "scattered among the nations" (for example, Deut. 4:25–31; 28:64–68; 30:1–10). Finally, sometime during the Babylonian exile, the book of Deuteronomy was separated from the books of Joshua through 2 Kings and now formed the end of the Pentateuch, or the Torah (Genesis through Deuteronomy).

The long process of reinterpretation that produced Deuteronomy presents us with a curious irony. On the one hand, our critical understanding of the book as the product of such a process suggests that contemporary interpreters within the church or synagogue have a warrant for imitating the process itself. In other words, just as the biblical authors reinterpreted old traditions in the light of current situations, so we need to reinterpret this ancient book in our own time and in the light of the rest of scripture. That may even entail changes or outright rejections of material that we find objectionable. For example, no one would want to punish rebellious teenagers by stoning them to death in public (Deut. 21:18–20; perhaps the front steps of a courthouse would be a location in present-day society corresponding to the ancient city gate). Similarly, we may find some of the dietary laws irrelevant. On a broader scale, we may denounce as inhuman the militant demands that all the Canaanite natives be slaughtered (as in

7:16). We may have problems accepting a religious model of government that our own ancestors replaced with the separation of church and state.

On the other hand, at several places the authors of the book appear to be thinking of their *own* reinterpretation as unchangeable, as when they have Moses say "you shall not add to the word which I command you, nor take from it" (4:2; compare 12:32). It is as if the editors were intentionally composing *scripture*. Yet such admonitions should not deter us from the responsibility of reinterpretation in our own time. Moreover, even passages that we might find objectionable may stimulate a fruitful theological debate regarding contemporary issues. For example, the command to kill all Canaanites is an extreme reaction against the opposite attitude (far more prevalent in Israelite history) in which the blending of Canaanite culture and religion with Israelite culture and religion threatened to erase any distinctions between the two. In other words, Deuteronomy 7 raises in sharp relief the perennial problem of the tension between religion and culture. On a lighter note, one also may occasionally find that otherwise obscure passages prove to be surprisingly relevant, as I once discovered when I presented the camp latrine rule (23:12–14) to an incredulous youth backpacking group!

Deuteronomy embraces different audiences, both hearers and readers. In its present form Deuteronomy is not so much a law code or even a treaty document as it is a series of farewell speeches. It is the testament of Moses, following a tradition associated with the death of other notable figures (Jacob, Gen. 47:29–49:33; compare Joshua, Josh. 23—24; David, 1 Kings 2:1–4). Moses is speaking to the second generation of Israelites who came out of Egypt, since virtually all the first generation, the lost generation of the wilderness, have died (Deut. 2:14–15). On this level, the past is the time of the exodus and the wilderness wandering; and the occupation of Canaan stands in the future.

When we think about the reinterpretations of Deuteronomy during the time of Hezekiah and Josiah, however, the events portrayed as future become part of the past. Israelites had been in the land for generations, and many of them had succumbed to the dangers of which Moses had warned. Thus warning becomes indictment; and, in the fall of the Northern Kingdom to the Assyrians (see 2 Kings 17), indictment has already moved to sentencing, a progression anticipated in the curses of the treaty (Deuteronomy 28).

When we think of the exilic edition of the book, the sense of doom pervades the entire work, and yet there is also a poignant glimmer of hope that beyond the grim reality of curse there stands the promise of renewed

blessing (as in 30:1–10). Moreover, when the Jewish community of the exile took the book from its place at the beginning of the Deuteronomistic
History (Joshua—2 Kings) and made it the last book of the Torah, Judaism's core scriptures (Genesis through Deuteronomy; see Neh. 8:1–8),
it thereby enhanced the accessibility of the book to *all* future generations,
certainly not only Jewish.

Deuteronomy suspends the reader—both ancient and modern—"on
Jordan's stormy banks," looking "with wishful eye" to "Canaan's fair and
happy land, where my possessions lie." The result is a tension between the
"already" and the "not yet" that invites—indeed, demands—wrenching
self-examination, whether of a nation's justice or of an individual's soul,
forcing the reader to hold past and future together as memory and hope.
This brings us to our fourth and final "r": responsibility.

RESPONDING TO THE TRADITION

A number of years ago, the Jewish community in New York City published a full-page ad in *The New York Times* on one of the major Jewish
holidays. The ad was a beautiful poem about the importance of religious
commitment, about sustaining a sense of community and maintaining justice. The poem was marked with a repeated refrain: "Once more, we stand
beneath the mountain." The phrase is a reference to the story of the giving of the Ten Commandments in Exodus (19:17), but it could apply
equally as well to the parallel account in Deuteronomy 4—5, and, indeed,
to all of Deuteronomy. "Once more, we stand beneath the mountain."

Partly because of its long and rich history of composition, Deuteronomy is imbued with a passionate summons to *responsibility*. The recalling
of stories and laws, the ratification of covenant, and the reinterpretation
of past traditions for new situations all have their primary purpose in the
demand that those who hear will respond appropriately. A deep urgency
runs throughout Moses' speeches and even throughout the laws.
Deuteronomy has been called "preached law," for Moses' speech is full of
emotion and frequently evokes feelings in his listeners that range from
tender love and compassion to outright terror. He is urging and motivat-
ing his listeners to obey the law. When Moses says, "You stand today all
of you before the Lord your God . . . that you may enter into the sworn
covenant" (Deut. 29:10, 12), the summons addresses the reader in a personal way, demanding a response one way or another. The authors are interested in nothing less than a reenactment of covenant commitment, with

all that that entails—primarily a pledge of allegiance to the Lord alone. All other loyalties are second to the love of God, and fair and compassionate dealings with one's neighbors are expected of everyone.

The sense of urgency in this summons is heightened throughout the book by the situation of the characters. Israel stands poised to go into the promised land, but Moses will not go with them. As Moses' final words, Deuteronomy is charged with a sense of crisis. Israel stands at a turning point that leads to either blessing or curse, life or death (Deut. 30:15–20). The authors, of course, hope that Israel will choose life, but the exilic editors know that Israel had finally chosen death. Thus the book is offered to all subsequent generations, who also "stand beneath the mountain," with the hope that they will choose the right path. When John Winthrop gave his sermon on board the *Arbella*, he selected precisely the right text from scripture. The authors of Deuteronomy no doubt would have approved.

PLEDGING ALLEGIANCE

It should now be clear that the book of Deuteronomy presents a *political* theology. It models its understanding of God and Israel in terms of a political treaty. The Lord is the Great King and Israel is the vassal. Accordingly, Deuteronomy itself, in large part, represents the polity of Israel, similar to the way that the Declaration of Independence and the Constitution represent the polity of the United States of America. That is, much of Deuteronomy represents the form of government of the realm of God. In interpreting this book one cannot separate the theological from the social and political without doing serious damage to Deuteronomy's meaning and significance.

One could summarize the theology of Deuteronomy by saying that it represents a sermonic and legal extension of the "two tables" of the Decalogue. The first part concerns allegiance to the Lord; the second concerns communal responsibility.

For the Deuteronomists no tradition out of Israel's past was more central than the opening lines of this treaty document: "I am the LORD your God, who brought you out of the land of Egypt, out of the house of slavery; you shall have no other gods before me" (Deut. 5:6–7). This one verse combines story and law. The historical prologue (story) of the treaty leads immediately to its most important stipulation (law). Because of the Lord's gracious act of salvation in the exodus from Egypt, Israel must now pledge allegiance to the Lord *alone* if the people want to continue within the Lord's protective sovereignty. The phrase "no other gods!" is the heart of Deuteronomic theology.

In the context of ancient Israel's history, "other gods" represented a literal threat to the Lord's exclusive claim on Israel. The wilderness traditions tell of Israel's succumbing to other gods even before entering Canaan, either in the form of the deity Baal, which means "lord," or in the form of the "golden calf" (compare Num. 25:1–9 and Deut. 4:3; Exod. 32, especially v. 4, and Deut. 9:6–10:11). Moreover, the subsequent history amply attests to the tendency of Israel to turn to the deities of the Canaanites after the occupation (as in Judg. 2:11–3:6).

This tendency only increased after the rise of the monarchy. Solomon, for example, built not only a temple for the Lord but also temples for the gods of each of his wives, and since he reportedly had seven hundred wives (as well as three hundred concubines), the temple architects must have been busy (1 Kings 11:1–8)! This report is undoubtedly exaggerated, but it indicates the inseparable connection between "religion" and "politics" in the ancient world. Solomon, like other kings, did not acquire numerous wives simply to satisfy his desire for female variety. Such marriages were political arrangements far more than romantic liaisons, part of the process of treaty making.

Thus Deuteronomy's wariness of intermarriage and treaty relationships with foreigners as leading inevitably to apostasy—that is, worship of other gods and breach of covenant (as in 7:1–6)—was rooted in historical fact. Today it would be easy to misunderstand the Deuteronomic polity as fanatical, authoritarian, and isolationist. In our culture, many people affirm religious pluralism, tolerate religious intermarriage, and applaud peaceful diplomatic relations between nations. Yet at the time of Deuteronomy, such seemingly virtuous cultural attitudes led quickly to forgetting Israel's historical identity and abandoning the Lord. The loss of communal memory and allegiance then undermined the people's character and threatened to rend the social fabric, a point to which we shall return shortly.

Most contemporary readers of Deuteronomy may at first think of the phrase "no other gods" as irrelevant to them. Perhaps a few Jews or Christians attracted to Zen meditation worry about worshiping the Buddha, but this is probably not the primary danger of contemporary apostasy. Rather, the danger more likely lies in the attribution of value and loyalty to secular powers, ranging from the national to the personal levels. Life is full of competing loyalties. No one is immune to them. No one grants exclusive loyalty to a single claimant. The question always has to do with which claimant receives the *highest* loyalty. Individuals may decide that success in a career demands their highest loyalty, subordinating the sometimes competing claims of family or community service. Nations may decide that military power demands their greatest investment, thereby subordinating other social needs. The claimant who receives our highest loyalty is, in effect, our god. Theologian Paul Tillich coined a phrase for such deities: Our god is our "ultimate concern" (see Tillich, *Dynamics of Faith*, 1957, chap. 1). Whenever that "ultimate concern" is someone or something other than the Lord, the God of Israel, then we too have fallen short of the Deuteronomist's warning—"no other gods!" As we shall see, perhaps the greatest temptation to worship "other gods" in our own time comes with the potentially conflicting loyalties of God and country (see the discussion of Deuteronomy 6, below).

PURSUING JUSTICE

If the first table of the Ten Commandments centers in allegiance to the Lord, the second centers in responsibility within the covenant community. The sabbath commandment (Deut. 5:12–15) illustrates this dual focus; indeed, it bridges nicely the theological with the social. Sabbath rest is to be observed in obedience to the command of the Lord. It has a natural function in providing a time for rejuvenation and relief from work. But the commandment extends beyond covenant members to include livestock, the "resident alien," and slaves, or, more accurately, indentured servants (see chap. 15). Indeed, the law is given *"so that"* the servants may rest along with the covenant members. Then the motivation follows: "Remember that *you* were a slave in the land of Egypt, and the LORD your God brought you out from there." Here we see how closely linked are loyalty to God, memory of the past, and responsibility to one's fellows.

The opening phrase of the Ten Commandments defines who Israel is, and, for that matter, who the Lord is: "I am the LORD your God, who brought you out of the land of Egypt" (Deut. 5:6). This narrative core of the community's identity is inextricably bound to the community's ethical character. The memory of the exodus story calls not only for loyalty to God, but also for responsibility to other people—the responsibility to ensure that the experience of liberation retold in the story is repeated within all levels of society, particularly among the disadvantaged. Memory is the basis of morality. In a word, the second focus of Deuteronomic theology is justice. "Justice, and only justice, you shall pursue" (16:20).

THE WAGES OF SIN

"No other gods!" "Justice, and only justice!" These are the two principal theological themes of the book. Over half a millennium later their dual centrality would be reaffirmed by the rabbis of first-century Judaism and in the teachings of Jesus, where the "great commandment" (a quotation from Deut. 6:4–5) would be supplemented with the "golden rule" (Lev. 19:18). Love of God and love of neighbor constitute the vertical and horizontal pillars of the covenant community. The result in Deuteronomy is a profoundly *social* ethic that concerns virtually every dimension of Israelite society, from sexual mores to sacral calendars. Within the covenant community, every individual act has a social consequence; every *individual* act of sin contains the potential for *national* disaster.

One of the most graphic illustrations of this corporate understanding appears in the law concerning an unsolved murder (Deut. 21:1–9). If a corpse is found outside a town, and no one knows who killed the person, an elaborate ritual is performed by the official representatives of the town—the elders, the judges, and the priests. The ritual includes the killing of a heifer, but the quasi-magical elements are displaced by the prayer for absolution directed to the Lord. The Deuteronomist believes that the taking of "innocent blood," if left unpunished, will infect the entire community with "bloodguilt," resulting in a communal disaster. Indeed, not just the local village is affected, but the entire people, as the prayer indicates (v. 8). Thus this ritual is intended to "purge the guilt of innocent blood from your midst." A similar phrase appears numerous other times within Deuteronomy 12—26, (as in 13:5—"so you shall purge the evil from your midst").

The social ethic of Deuteronomy would thus approve of the contemporary proverb, "one rotten apple spoils the barrel." Indeed, in a speech following the long list of curses that are threatened for breach of covenant, Moses warns of the irresponsible individual who thinks that his or her own wrongful act will go unpunished (Deut. 29:18–28). While at one point it appears that God would "single out" this individual for punishment (v. 21), the rest of the passage shows clearly that the entire people would be engulfed with the curse, "the whole land" destroyed like Sodom and Gomorrah (v. 23) and the people carried off into exile (v. 28).

That individual acts can carry negative consequences for generations is part of the social reality enshrined in the Decalogue itself, where God threatens to punish "children for the iniquity of parents, to the third and fourth generation" (Deut. 5:9). While we may be uncomfortable with ascribing such punishment to God, few can deny that in families, larger social groups, and even nations, one generation often suffers because of the former's wrongdoing. Moreover, for the Deuteronomist, the imposition of punishment on an entire community ("moist and dry alike," 29:19) was simply a commonplace in the relations between political powers, and, again, was legally mandated by the curses of treaties. One need only read the annals of Assyrian kings to realize how brutally thorough the destruction of rebellious vassals could be (Pritchard, *Texts*, 1969, 274–300).

The severity of the consequences of individual acts of injustice is thus matched by the severity of sanctions. Deuteronomy sometimes prescribes the most radical prevention—destruction of the rotten apple. If, in Israel's view, an individual's breach of covenant will bring down the Lord's curse on the whole people, then there is little alternative but expulsion or even death. Nowhere is the severity more apparent than in the case of the execution of the rebellious son, to which I have already referred (Deut. 21:18–20). Again we hear, "so you shall purge the evil from your midst."

While we may rightly reject this law as barbaric, we may also do well to ponder the *social value system* of which it is an extreme example. Because Deuteronomy presents a *political* theology, it has no place for a type of individualism in which personal actions are divorced from the communal good. The purpose of human life is not simply personal success but the attainment and maintenance of a just social order. Deuteronomy is interested in achieving the "great society," not in the great achievements of individuals. Its emphasis is on the interest of the community as a whole, not self-interest (or even "interest groups"). Its primary concern is for the public good, not private gain.

Thus Deuteronomy represents a social ethic strongly at odds with contemporary culture, at least, American culture. In the latter, "the individual is prior to society, which comes into existence only through the voluntary contract of individuals trying to maximize their own self-interest . . . the self has become the main form of reality." The quotation is from a book that would serve as an instructive companion to the book of Deuteronomy: *Habits of the Heart: Individualism and Commitment in American Life* by Robert Bellah and others. To say that in contemporary culture the self "has become the main form of reality" is to put into contemporary sociological language what Deuteronomy means by "serving other gods."

When the center of value, or "ultimate concern," shifts away from God and away from community to the individual self, the result is a disintegration of both authentic human nature (which the Bible insists is inherently communal) and the social fabric. This is why, for the Deuteronomist, "serving other gods" was not simply a theological problem (strictly construed) but a profoundly social problem. Historical experience proved that the loss of the community's center of value in the Lord and in the covenant community spawned social decay, the latter exhibited primarily by the increase of power and wealth for the upper elements of Israelite society and oppression and injustice for the lower. When Amos condemned the upper-crust women of Samaria for ignoring the poor while enjoying the luxuries of privilege (Amos 4:1), he was speaking in the same spirit that animates much of Deuteronomy.

A MORAL VIEW OF HISTORY

A political theology with a social ethic thus produced a moral view of history. The nation is the recipient of rewards or the victim of punishments, depending on the adequacy of the national character. "If you will only obey the LORD your God, by diligently observing all his commandments . . . all these blessings shall come upon you" (Deut. 28:1–2), "but if you will not obey the LORD your God by diligently observing all his commandments . . . then all these curses shall come upon you" (28:15). This strict moral system not only permeates Deuteronomy but is the driving force behind much of the Deuteronomistic History (Joshua—2 Kings). The commentary on the fall of the Northern Kingdom in 2 Kings 17 provides a graphic example: "This occurred because the people of Israel had sinned against the LORD their God, who had brought them up out of the land of Egypt" (v. 7; a long exposition of the sins follows). Similar commentary can be found in every part of the history, from Joshua to 2 Kings. Moreover, the same moral view of history informs the prophets and can be seen (in far less political contexts) in the wisdom literature of Proverbs.

It is easy to find fault with the Deuteronomic theology of history. It implies a neat and tidy moral system that both history and personal experience often prove wrong. This is especially true when the theology is applied in reverse, as it were—that is, when disasters such as famine or plague, or military defeat (28:17–25) are interpreted automatically to be signs of divine punishment and therefore of human sin. The other side of the coin—when prosperity is interpreted to be a sign of divine reward for human righteousness—can be equally dangerous. The first understanding can produce a kind of masochistic theology; the second, the "gospel of success." Fortunately, the canon includes works that are critical of such simplistic views of life—Job and Ecclesiastes—particularly when the *political* theology of Deuteronomy is applied indiscriminately to *individual* suffering.

Careful study of Deuteronomy will also disclose a theology that is often far more subtle than a simple rewards-and-punishment system would suggest. For example, Deuteronomy 8 interprets national prosperity not as a sign of divine reward, much less as an indication of human achievement, but as a gift from God, and one that leads easily to forgetting the community's story and thus turning affluence into a lethal spiritual poverty.

Preoccupation with the weaknesses of Deuteronomy's moral view of history should not allow us to ignore its strengths. The primary motivation behind the communal ethic is grateful memory of the past, not the desire for reward or the fear of punishment. The covenant people are summoned to live a particular way because of who they are, not because of what they want to obtain or avoid. The primary purpose of this ethic is provision for the public good, the setting of boundaries within which the covenant community can exist with integrity and social responsibility. The primary judgment of this ethic is that communal amnesia and social injustice become cancerous growths within the public body and will eventually destroy the body. Despite the problems one might have with perspectives in this book that is almost three thousand years old, any contemporary society that abandons the foregoing ethical principles does so to its peril.

THE JOY OF THE TORAH

It would be unfortunate if the preceding overview of Deuteronomic theology left the impression that the book is full of gloom and doom and not much else. It is true that its authors intended Deuteronomy to be read with the utmost seriousness, indeed, with a sense of anguish. A historian who uses as his opening chapter the story of a national disaster, itself caused by a foolish disregard for the past, is hardly pandering to cockeyed optimists (Deut. 1:19–46). Indeed, the model for an appropriate reading of Deuteronomy is provided within the Deuteronomistic History itself in the figure of the pious king Josiah: "When the king heard the words of the book of the law, he tore his clothes," a symbolic gesture of mourning and repentance (2 Kings 22:11). In contrast, consider the later king Jehoiakim, who heard similar words from the prophet Jeremiah, also read from a scroll. Yet he did not tear a single thread from his purple robe, but burned the scroll, piece by piece (Jer. 36:23–24). The Deuteronomic school, which had much in common with Jeremiah, clearly wanted its readers to follow the example of Josiah. Repentance—a complete "turning around" of one's attitude and behavior—is the primary response that the authors wish.

The emphasis on repentance, however, should not obscure one of the other dominant moods in Deuteronomy, namely, joy. Jewish tradition has a festival called *simhat torah*, which means "rejoicing over Torah." In this festival, the participants parade around the synagogue holding the sacred scroll of the Torah (the first five books of the Old Testament) over their heads, dancing and singing for joy. This festival, which continues to this day, has its roots in the Deuteronomic understanding of God's will for Israel. At the beginning and at the end of the law code (Deut. 12:7, 12, 18; and 26:11, respectively), as well as in between (14:26; 16:11, 14), Israel is told to "rejoice" or "celebrate." While the gift of a bounteous land and its harvests is sometimes the immediate cause for celebration (14:26; 16:11, 14), in the end Israel is also called to "rejoice in all the good which the Lord your God has given to you" (26:11, RSV). For Deuteronomy, this gift of grace also includes the law itself. The giving of the law is an expression of God's love; thus obedience to the law is a joyful act of love in response.

Deuteronomy agrees with the psalmist who writes, "the precepts of the Lord are right, rejoicing the heart" (Psalms 19:8). In its broadest sense, the Hebrew word *torah* means "guidance" or "instruction." In its most narrow sense, it can refer to a specific law. Just as a parent provides guidance for a child, so the Lord provides guidance for Israel. This guidance is loving and protective, even if at times it may be strict and even difficult (Deut. 8:1–5). Because this guidance is an expression of God's benevolence, it is gracious. Similarly, just as a child experiences delight in following a parent's guidance, so Israel may experience delight in following the Lord's guidance. Thus both the giving and the receiving of torah are gestures of love and joy. That the authors are well aware of the more frequently exhibited attitude of *dis*obedience makes their appeal to the joy of torah all the more realistic (see 9:7).

When we combine this sense of joyful giving and response with the *political* dimensions of the law, that is, as the polity of the covenant people, the grace of torah appears even more profound. Because God's guidance is given in specific laws that regulate behavior within the community, providing for justice, the joy that the torah makes possible is nothing less than that of a community at peace (Hebrew *shalom*), in the deepest sense of the Hebrew word—"wholeness." Deuteronomy has a vision of a community at peace with God and with each other. To this extent, Deuteronomy represents a biblical utopia. Perhaps the most poignant glimpse of this vision occurs in the economic legislation of chapter 15, where God says, "there will . . . be no one in need among you . . . if only you will obey the LORD your God" (vv. 4, 5).

Christians who read Deuteronomy should thus remember that it was written (at its latest edition) half a millennium before Paul and the New Testament. What Paul understood "the law" to mean in the first century C.E. may not necessarily have been the same as what the original authors thought it meant (nor, for that matter, the way later Jews would interpret it). The same caution is in order for the controversies in the Gospels and the statements that Jesus makes about the law. When Paul talks about "the law of sin and death" (Rom. 8:2; see 7:5, 8), or when Jesus breaks the sabbath law and argues with the Pharisees over its meaning (as in Mark 2: 23–28), what "the law" means theologically must be determined in the context of first-century debates between the early Christian and Jewish communities, and not read automatically into the book of Deuteronomy. It is also worth remembering that the Gospels represent Jesus positively as the *fulfillment* of the law (especially Matt. 5:17–20), and that, when asked for the "great commandment," Jesus responded precisely the way that Deuteronomy would suggest by citing the "creed" of Deuteronomy 6:4–5 and adding to it the law of the neighbor from Leviticus 19:18.

Although the term "gospel" derives from Christian tradition, it would even be appropriate theologically to say that Deuteronomy sees the law *as* "gospel." Since the covenant law is an expression of divine love and provides the parameters for the "peaceable kingdom," it is received and celebrated as "good news." The law provides the means by which the redeemed people of the exodus may become the sanctified community of the covenant. Indeed, the people's salvation is incomplete without this sanctification, just as freedom from tyranny is incomplete without a new constitution to prevent a new tyranny.

An analogy from recent American history may be helpful. The civil rights movement of the 1950s and early 1960s was a freedom movement, but the accomplishments of the various demonstrations and marches were not fully realized until the movement's demands for justice were translated into law—the Civil Rights Act of 1964. The adoption of that legislation was a cause for celebration, for *simhat torah*. More specifically, when an African American could *legally* ride in the front of a bus, the law itself could be seen as an agent of continuing redemption within the community, and thus a source of joy.

GRACE AND REPENTANCE

The note of doom that sounds throughout the book of Deuteronomy is also tempered by a hope based not on the people's responsibility but on God's unconditional grace. From beginning to end, Deuteronomy directs Israel's memory not only to the giving of the law and the liberation from Egypt, but also to God's oath sworn to the "fathers," the promise of land and nationhood (see Deut. 1:8–10 and 34:4). The reference is to the stories of Genesis in which this promise is made to Abraham and Sarah and then to subsequent generations.

The Deuteronomists refer to this promise in two critical contexts. First, in the retelling of the story of the golden calf (Deut. 9:8–10:5), God's threat to destroy the people because of their sin, that is, to exercise the curse of the treaty (9:13), is countered by Moses' appeal to God's promise to the ancestors (9:25–27). The result is a reinstitution of the covenant community. Second, in passages posed in the future but almost certainly within the author's past, a description of national defeat and exile stops just short of despair by the invocation of the promise to the ancestors. Even though the people may be "scattered among the nations," they will not be without hope, "because the LORD your God is a merciful God, he will neither abandon you nor destroy you; he will not forget the covenant with your ancestors that he swore to them" (4:27, 31; see 30:4–5).

The unconditionality of this covenant with the ancestors and its function as the bedrock of hope are related theologically to the traditions of the covenant with the house of David. In the latter traditions too we hear of a promise that will last forever, an oath as enduring as the sun. Even when the commandments of this covenant are broken, punishment will not entail a mutual breaking of the divine commitment, an end to God's "steadfast love" (see Psalms 89:28–38). Like the note of doom, this note of hope rings throughout the historical books beginning with its announcement in 2 Samuel 7 (as in vv. 11–16; see 1 Kings 11:34–36; 15:3–4; 2 Kings 8:18–19). Indeed, this hope in the promise to David can be maintained even in the face of its apparent failure (see the rest of Psalm 89 beginning at v. 38).

Deuteronomy invokes the promises to the ancestors in order to point beyond the promises themselves to a fundamental aspect of God's character, namely, God's unconditional love for Israel. This love is the source of Israel's election, beginning in the ancient past with Abraham and Sarah, and stretching into the distant future. Israel is not loved because of some intrinsic quality, or even because of obedience to God—God loves Israel simply because that is the way God *is* (Deut. 7:7–8). This love is unearned and, indeed, undeserved, and it is Israel's last redoubt.

When we juxtapose the appeals to God's unconditional love with the demands for corporate responsibility, an inescapable tension appears. On the one hand, Deuteronomy calls for righteousness and threatens disaster if the demand is not met. On the other hand, when Israel's disobedience reaches its fullest extent, both in the past (chaps. 9—10) and in the future (chaps. 4 and 30), the disaster is mitigated by God's grace.

The authors are wrestling with a theological problem here that is by no means limited to ancient Israel, much less to Deuteronomy. They want to pose the requirement of ethical responsibility with utmost seriousness, yet they are not willing ultimately to leave human beings to suffer the full consequences of their own *ir*responsibility. They want God's demand for "justice and only justice" to be the determinative factor in the people's fate, yet their history tells them of the same God whose love at critical times overrides Israel's failure to heed this demand. They want to maintain that human beings are free moral agents, capable of doing what they should do, and that the demands placed upon them are realistic (Deut. 30:11–14). Yet they must recognize that human beings are incorrigibly stubborn and that their failure of will can lead to corporate suicide if divine wrath does not give way to divine mercy. Thus at times it is not clear whether hope is based on an act of human repentance or repentance itself is based on trust in the assurance of mercy (as in 4:29–31).

Again, the tension is not peculiar to Deuteronomy. It is shared with a prophet like Hosea, who saw with painful accuracy the inner conflict between God's love and anger (Hosea 11). It is reflected in Jesus' parable of the prodigal son (Luke 15:11–32), where we cannot finally separate the son's decision to "return" and the father's already open arms. The same tension appears between a parable like that of the unforgiving servant (Matt. 18:21–35) and a story like that of the woman caught in adultery (John 8:1–11).

Within Deuteronomy, the tension is one that the authors refuse to resolve. Indeed, the two sides of the tension again can be understood to reflect the different times and audiences that the book addressed: At one time, a nation on the brink of disaster, called desperately to repentance; then, once that disaster has arrived, a nation offered the hope of a future rooted only in the unconditional love of God. Here again the book as a whole reflects the prophetic movement and the shift observable within the prophetic books from a message of judgment to a message of hope. For example, note the shift at the end of the book of Amos and the appeal to the Davidic promise in Amos 9:11–15. If pushed too far, the emphasis on responsibility turns God into a rigid moralistic system, a merciless divine accountant, for whom the "bottom line" of human sins is all that counts. If unconditional love is pushed too far, it becomes "cheap grace," a phrase coined by German Lutheran pastor Dietrich Bonhoeffer, under which no repentance is necessary, no responsibility required, and one may "continue in sin that grace may abound" (Rom. 6:1).

When the exilic community severed the book of Deuteronomy from its place at the beginning of Israel's history in the books of Joshua through Kings, and designated it as the end of the Pentateuch, it lifted up the "presentness" of the text and ensured its powerful applicability for all subsequent generations. Moses' final testament leaves Israel completely prepared for the crossing of the Jordan, but the fulfillment of the people's destiny remains an adventure dependent on how well they have absorbed that preparation. Deuteronomy (and thus the Torah) leave the characters poised at the moment of departure, not at the moment of arrival. The goal of the promised land lies ahead, not behind. The reality of a covenant community of justice and peace exists in theory, but not in practice. The story of God's relationship to humankind from the creation of the world is suspended at this moment, awaiting the response of that people chosen as the primary agent of that story (see 4:32–40). What will the outcome be? The answer lies with Israel.

We began with John Winthrop's speech on board the *Arbella*, and with contemporary pilgrims singing the hymn "On Jordan's Stormy Banks I Stand." Perhaps the most captivating quality of Deuteronomy is its perennial ability to engage the modern reader. It is almost impossible to read this book and not, at some point, to identify with the characters, both individually and corporately. We too stand "on Jordan's stormy banks." Like ancient Israel, we too are invited to recall God's marvelous deeds, to ratify a covenant offered to us, to reinterpret the old stories, where necessary, and to heed the demand to live responsibly as a community of justice and peace. We too are summoned to "choose this day" whom we will serve and how we will live. Deuteronomy provides the *torah*, the "guidance," for that decision. Even modern readers would do well to follow it.

SCOPE OF THIS BOOK

Before we turn to the opening chapters of Deuteronomy, a few words about the scope of this book are in order. Restrictions on space do not allow for lengthy discussion of many passages, or the inclusion of the whole text of Deuteronomy. In these instances, brief notes are included. Chapters 1 through 8 deal with the prologue material in Deuteronomy 1—11. Chapters 2 through 5 focus on the Ten Commandments in Deuteronomy 5:6–21 and the closely related material surrounding this unit, including the framework of Deuteronomy 5 and Deuteronomy 6 and 7.

Chapters 9 through 12 discuss some of the specific laws included in the "statutes and ordinances" of the covenant. Here the limitations of space are most evident. The discussion focuses on those laws that best illustrate Deuteronomy's theological and ethical concerns. However, the commentary elsewhere often refers to passages within the legal corpus (Deuteronomy 12—26), and the reader may consult these passages for supplementary study. Chapters 13 through 15, focus on the end of the legal corpus, the completion of covenant making, and the heritage of Deuteronomy within our own communities of faith.

1. D-Day or Doomsday?
Deuteronomy 1:1–4:40

Imagine yourself reading the first chapter of a new history of the United States of America. The opening paragraphs describe several scenes from the 1960s and early 1970s: the last United States helicopter lifting off the roof of the embassy in Saigon, escaping from the victorious Viet Cong; the funeral processions of John and Robert Kennedy, and of Martin Luther King Jr.; the Senate "Watergate" hearings on the impeachment of President Richard Nixon. What would the placement of these scenes at the beginning suggest about the author's approach to American history? It would certainly suggest a historical perspective that was critical and sober, not given to flattery or unrestrained flag-waving. It might even suggest a perspective that was gloomy and pessimistic.

We find just such a perspective in the opening chapter of Deuteronomy. A familiar proverb says that those who will not learn from history are doomed to repeat it. Deuteronomy opens with a story of doom in the hopes of preventing such repetition.

BEYOND THE JORDAN
Deuteronomy 1:1–25

1:1 These are the words that Moses spoke to all Israel beyond the Jordan—in the wilderness, on the plain opposite Suph, between Paran and Tophel, Laban, Hazeroth, and Di-zahab. ² (By the way of Mount Seir it takes eleven days to reach Kadesh-barnea from Horeb.) ³ In the fortieth year, on the first day of the eleventh month, Moses spoke to the Israelites just as the LORD had commanded him to speak to them. ⁴ This was after he had defeated King Sihon of the Amorites, who reigned in Heshbon, and King Og of Bashan, who reigned in Ashtaroth and in Edrei. ⁵ Beyond the Jordan in the land of Moab, Moses undertook to expound this law as follows:

⁶ The LORD our God spoke to us at Horeb, saying, "You have stayed long enough at this mountain. ⁷ Resume your journey, and go into the hill country of the Amorites as well as into the neighboring regions—the Arabah, the hill country, the Shephelah, the Negeb, and the seacoast—the land of the Canaanites and the Lebanon, as far as the great river, the river Euphrates. ⁸ See, I have set the land before you; go in and take possession of the land that I swore to your ancestors, to Abraham, to Isaac, and to Jacob, to give to them and to their descendents after them."

⁹ At that time I said to you, "I am unable by myself to bear you. ¹⁰ The LORD your God has multiplied you, so that today you are as numerous as the stars of heaven. ¹¹ May the LORD, the God of your ancestors, increase you a thousand times more and bless you, as he has promised you! ¹² But how can I bear the heavy burden of your disputes all by myself? ¹³ Choose for each of your tribes individuals who are wise, discerning, and reputable to be your leaders." ¹⁴ You answered me, "The plan you have proposed is a good one." ¹⁵ So I took the leaders of your tribes, wise and reputable individuals, and installed them as leaders over you, commanders of thousands, commanders of hundreds, commanders of fifties, commanders of tens, and officials, throughout your tribes. ¹⁶ I charged your judges at that time: "Give the members of your community a fair hearing, and judge rightly between one person and another, whether citizen or resident alien. ¹⁷ You must not be partial in judging: hear out the small and the great alike; you shall not be intimidated by anyone, for the judgment is God's. Any case that is too hard for you, bring to me, and I will hear it." ¹⁸ So I charged you at that time with all the things that you should do.

¹⁹ Then, just as the LORD our God had ordered us, we set out from Horeb and went through all that great and terrible wilderness that you saw, on the way to the hill country of the Amorites, until we reached Kadesh-barnea. ²⁰ I said to you, "You have reached the hill country of the Amorites, which the LORD our God is giving us. ²¹ See, the LORD your God has given the land to you; go up, take possession, as the LORD, the God of your ancestors, has promised you; do not fear or be dismayed."

²² All of you came to me and said, "Let us send men ahead of us to explore the land for us and bring back a report to us regarding the route by which we should go up and the cities we will come to." ²³ The plan seemed good to me, and I selected twelve of you, one from each tribe. ²⁴ They set out and went up into the hill country, and when they reached the Valley of Eshcol they spied it out ²⁵ and gathered some of the land's produce, which they brought down to us. They brought back a report to us, and said, "It is a good land that the LORD our God is giving us."

Deuteronomy 1:1–5 provides the dramatic setting of the book. The time is the fortieth year after the exodus of the Hebrew slaves from Egypt;

the place is "beyond the Jordan, in the wilderness," that is, on the east bank of the Jordan River, looking over to Canaan. Moses' audience stands in time and place at the boundary between the wilderness and the promised land. The setting at the border easily becomes a spiritual metaphor, inviting the author's audience to consider its own situation and the extent to which that situation conforms to or departs from the Israel in the story.

At the end of the narrator's introduction in verse 5, Moses' speech is described as "law" (that is, *torah*). The word can refer to specific legal prohibitions or requirements, as it does in much of Deuteronomy 12—26, but it also can mean "guidance" in a more general sense. Here it clearly includes the repetition of stories from the past as well as Moses' commentary on those stories. Yet something of the imperative force of "law" resides in this exposition of narrative—the retelling of these stories from the past directs or *commands* how Israel is to live in the present.

Moses' speech now begins in 1:6 and continues through 4:40. Despite the singular power of chapter 1, the editors have indicated a continuous unit running until the end of the speech in 4:40, where the narrator reappears. We can outline the unit as narrative point (1:9–46), narrative counterpoint (2:1–3:22), narrative conclusion (3:23–29), and commentary (4:1–40), while recognizing that narration and admonition are inextricably intertwined.

Moses takes his audience back in time to the departure of the exodus generation from Horeb (= Sinai), after receiving the covenant stipulations. The stories that follow represent alternative versions to those in the book of Numbers (departure from Sinai and appointment of officers, in Numbers 10—11, the defeat at Kadesh-barnea in Numbers 13—14). That the generation who came out of Egypt is not the same as Moses' audience is the burden of the following stories. Yet the two generations are in similar situations—on the verge of the promised land. Just as the story of the past recalls that time when the exodus generation was poised to enter the land, so the story of the present generation portrays their children poised to cross the Jordan. Indeed, we can identify at least four different "Israels" as we read Deuteronomy 1—11: (1) the exodus generation, (2) the new generation (Moses' audience), (3) the author's audience (itself multiple, since there are several authors), and (4) contemporary readers of faith who also identify themselves as the "Israel of God." We become the "you" to whom Moses speaks, and we are challenged to ask ourselves in what sense we too stand "beyond the Jordan," and what is required of us if we would enter the promised land.

Moses' opening words are the words of the Lord, and they are full of promise. God tells them that the time to enter Canaan has arrived and describes the land in terms of ideal boundaries never historically realized. The reference to the oath to the ancestors in 1:8 ties this moment not only to the story of Exodus but also to that of Genesis. The time of fulfillment of the promises made long ago to Abraham is at hand—"Go . . . to the land that I will show you" (Gen. 12:1). God has placed the land before Israel, much as a gift is placed before its recipient. All that Israel needs to do is to unwrap the gift. The land is theirs for the taking. The following passage, Deuteronomy 1:9–18, continues the emphasis on promises fulfilled. Moses must appoint administrative, military, and judicial assistants because the people have become a "great nation" "as numerous as the stars of heaven" (Gen. 12:1; 15:5; 22:17).

The next passage, Deuteronomy 1:19–25, portrays the people's initial obedience to the divine command. They pass through the wilderness and come to Kadesh-barnea, the "staging area" for the conquest of the land of Canaan. Moses reiterates the gift of the land, adding an encouragement that is typical of military rhetoric: "Do not fear or be dismayed" (v. 21; compare 20:1–4). Then, in a move that seems prudent, the people suggest that spies be sent ahead. Moses approves, and the spies return bearing some fruit of the land and declaring that God's gift is good indeed.

REVEILLE TO RETREAT
Deuteronomy 1:26–45

1:26 **But you were unwilling to go up. You rebelled against the command of the LORD your God;** 27 **you grumbled in your tents and said, "It is because the LORD hates us that he has brought us out of the land of Egypt, to hand us over to the Amorites to destroy us.** 28 **Where are we headed? Our kindred have made our hearts melt by reporting, 'The people are stronger and taller than we; the cities are large and fortified up to heaven! We actually saw there the offspring of the Anakim!' "** 29 **I said to you, "Have no dread or fear of them.** 30 **The LORD your God, who goes before you, is the one who will fight for you, just as he did for you in Egypt before your very eyes,** 31 **and in the wilderness, where you saw how the LORD your God carried you, just as one carries a child, all the way that you traveled until you reached this place.** 32 **But in spite of this, you have no trust in the LORD your God,** 33 **who goes before you on the way to seek out a place for you to camp, in fire by night, and in the cloud by day, to show you the route you should take."**

34 **When the LORD heard your words, he was wrathful and swore:** 35 **"Not one of these—not one of this evil generation—shall see the good land that I swore to give to your ancestors,** 36 **except Caleb son of Jephun-**

neh. He shall see it, and to him and to his descendants I will give the land on which he set foot, because of his complete fidelity to the LORD." [37] Even with me the LORD was angry on your account, saying, "You also shall not enter there. [38] Joshua son of Nun, your assistant, shall enter there; encourage him, for he is the one who will secure Israel's possession of it. [39] And as for your little ones, who you thought would become booty, your children, who today do not yet know right from wrong, they shall enter there; to them I will give it, and they shall take possession of it. [40] But as for you, journey back into the wilderness, in the direction of the Red Sea."

[41] You answered me, "We have sinned against the LORD! We are ready to go up and fight, just as the LORD our God commanded us." So all of you strapped on your battle gear, and thought it easy to go up into the hill country. [42] The LORD said to me, "Say to them, 'Do not go up and do not fight, for I am not in the midst of you; otherwise you will be defeated by your enemies.' " [43] Although I told you, you would not listen. You rebelled against the command of the LORD and presumptuously went up into the hill country. [44] The Amorites who lived in that hill country then came out against you and chased you as bees do. They beat you down in Seir as far as Hormah. [45] When you returned and wept before the LORD, the LORD would neither heed your voice nor pay you any attention.

Unexpectedly and inexplicably, the people balk at the very moment that victory seems to be theirs. The bugle sounds, but no one joins the charge. Deuteronomy 1:26–33, the passage that describes the people's rebellion, is full of irony, and the arrangement of the story focuses our attention not on the people's action (or lack thereof) but on their attitude. Moses reports their rebellion in shocking terms: "You grumbled . . . 'because the LORD hates us . . . he has brought us out of Egypt.' "

In the narrative context this accusation is an irrational and spiteful distortion of the *love* of God, employing the expression that usually *praises* God (see 7:8). The exodus is attributed to divine malice! The promise of victory previously announced is turned upside down into a threat of destruction. The irony is most profound when the people say that their hearts have "melted." This is military rhetoric that usually refers to the fear of the *enemy* in the face of the Lord's mighty army (see Josh. 2:9, 11; 5:1; 7:5). Moses uses similar language in his response, reminding them of the God who fought for them against the Egyptians, brought them through the wilderness, and went before them in a pillar of cloud and fire (see Exod. 13:21–22; 14:13–14, 19–20, 24–25). Yet in spite of this historical reminder, the people refuse to take the gift of the land. Why is this?

Embedded in the story is a detail that provides a partial answer: there are giants in the land! And they live in impregnable castles! These are the

"Anakim," fierce warriors who stood some thirteen feet high, making the later Goliath seem small (see Deut. 3:11; 9:1–3; 1 Samuel 4). The "fine print" in the spies' report has come out, and it is intimidating.

But the way in which the author has woven this report into his retelling of the story produces a masterful effect (contrast Num. 13:27–28). By delaying its inclusion, separating it from the good news of the land's fruitfulness, he has created the impression that the people's resistance is unfounded and shameful. The people seem to rebel before they hear the negative intelligence. As a result, our attention shifts from the report to its reception, from the bad news to the way the people *handle* the bad news. In short, the story focuses on one of the fundamental concerns of Deuteronomy—the attitude of the people's hearts. They had nothing to fear but fear itself, yet their hearts melted. The problem is not the power of the giants but the weakness of the people's faith. Despite all the evidence of God's previous faithfulness, they "have no trust in the LORD" (Deut. 1:32).

The rest of the story, Deuteronomy 1:34–40, is sadder still. As a result of the people's rebellion, God forbids any of them to enter the land, except for Caleb, who had resisted the rebellion (see Num. 13:30; 14:6–9). Only the children too young to rebel will be allowed to enter; the rest are doomed to wander in the wilderness until they die, a sentence that is completed in Deuteronomy 2:14–15. Even Moses is forbidden to enter the land because of the people's rebellion (1:37; see the discussion, below, on 3:23–28). God is capable of irony as well, for the children who survive are those whose death the people feared, and the direction in which they are now sent is not Canaan but the Red Sea—as if they are going back to Egypt!

Finally, the people realize their mistake too late (vv. 41–45). As suddenly penitent as they were rebellious, they vow to join the battle, yet Moses warns them that God is no longer with them. They persist, and now it is their careless combativeness that constitutes rebellion (v. 43). The result is defeat and retreat. What had promised to be D-Day ended up being doomsday.

In effect, Deuteronomy 2 and 3 represent a reversal of the preceding story of defeat—doomsday becomes D-Day.

DOOMSDAY BECOMES D-DAY
Deuteronomy 1:46–2:9; 2:13–35

1:46 **After you had stayed at Kadesh as many days as you did,** 2:1 **we journeyed back into the wilderness, in the direction of the Red Sea, as the LORD** had told me and skirted Mount Seir for many days. 2 Then the LORD said to me: 3 "You have been skirting this hill country long enough. Head north, 4 and charge the people as follows: You are about to pass through the territory of your kindred, the descendants of Esau, who live in Seir. They will be afraid of you, so, be very careful 5 not to engage in battle with them, for I will not give you even so much as a foot's length of their land, since I have given Mount Seir to Esau as a possession. 6 You shall purchase food from them for money, so that you may eat; and you shall also buy water from them for money, so that you may drink. 7 Surely the LORD your God has blessed you in all your undertakings; he knows your going through this great wilderness. These forty years the LORD your God has been with you; you have lacked nothing." 8 So we passed by our kin, the descendents of Esau who live in Seir, leaving behind the route of the Arabah, and leaving behind Elath and Ezion-geber.

When we had headed out along the route of the wilderness of Moab, 9 the LORD said to me: "Do not harass Moab or engage them in battle, for I will not give you any of its land as a possession, since I have given Ar as a possession to the descendants of Lot . . . . 13 Now then, proceed to cross over the Wadi Zered."

So we crossed over the Wadi Zered. 14 And the length of time we had traveled from Kadesh-barnea until we crossed the Wadi Zered was thirty-eight years, until the entire generation of warriors had perished from the camp, as the LORD had sworn concerning them. 15 Indeed, the LORD's own hand was against them, to root them out from the camp, until all had perished.

16 Just as soon as all the warriors had died off from among the people, 17 the LORD spoke to me, saying, 18 "Today you are going to cross the boundary of Moab at Ar. 19 When you approach the frontier of the Ammonites, do not harass them or engage them in battle, for I will not give the land of the Ammonites to you as a possession, because I have given it to the descendants of Lot . . . . 24 "Proceed on your journey and cross the Wadi Arnon. See, I have handed over to you King Sihon the Amorite of Heshbon, and his land. Begin to take possession by engaging him in battle. 25 This day I will begin to put the dread and fear of you upon the peoples everywhere under heaven; when they hear report of you, they will tremble and be in anguish because of you."

26 So I sent messengers from the wilderness of Kedemoth to King Sihon of Heshbon with the following terms of peace: 27 "If you let me pass through your land, I will travel only along the road; I will turn aside neither to the right nor to the left. 28 You shall sell me food for money, so that I may eat, and supply me water for money, so that I may drink. Only allow me to pass through on foot—29 just as the descendants of Esau who live in Seir have done for me and likewise the Moabites who live in Ar—until I cross the Jor-

dan into the land that the LORD our God is giving us." [30] **But King Sihon of Heshbon was not willing to let us pass through, for the LORD your God had hardened his spirit and made his heart defiant in order to hand him over to you, as he has now done.**

[31] **The LORD said to me, "See, I have begun to give Sihon and his land over to you. Begin now to take possession of his land."** [32] **So when Sihon came out against us, he and all his people for battle at Jahaz,** [33] **the LORD our God gave him over to us; and we struck him down, along with his off-spring and all his people.** [34] **At that time we captured all his towns, and in each town we utterly destroyed men, women, and children. We left not a single survivor.** [35] **Only the livestock we kept as spoil for ourselves, as well as the plunder of the towns that we had captured.**

(The remaining material, 2:36–3:22, contains a similar report about conquering King Og of Bashan, then a report on the distribution of land east of the Jordan and Moses' order that the East Jordanian tribes help the others in conquering the land west of the Jordan.)

Just as the previous story began with God's command to turn toward Canaan, so does this one (compare Deut. 2:3 with 1:6–7), but what follows is a story of complete obedience. God orders that Israel pass through the lands of Edom and Moab and Ammon, purchasing provisions when neces-sary but in no way threatening or fighting with these peoples (2:1–19). The reason for this peaceful approach is that these people are "kindred" folk, that is, they are related to the ancestors of Israel. The Edomites derive from Esau, the estranged brother of Jacob, and the Moabites and Ammonites de-rive from Lot, Abraham's nephew (Gen. 18:30–38).

Now Israel finally begins the assault on the Amorites with the defeat of Sihon and Og. Moses distributes their lands east of the Jordan to several Israelite tribes, whose warriors will nonetheless be required to participate in the conquest of Canaan (Deut. 2:24–3:23). Israel has indeed begun to take possession of the promised land. Thus the story of rebellion and de-feat in chapter 1 is balanced by stories of obedience and victory in chap-ters 2—3, presenting two radically different possibilities for the present generation who stand "beyond the Jordan."

BETWEEN LITERALISM AND ALLEGORY
Deuteronomy 1:1–3:22

We now pause for a moment to raise some difficult questions. How shall the contemporary Christian interpret these stories of conquest? If we are implicitly included in the "you" addressed by Moses and the author, what do the other characters represent for us, especially the enemies of Israel? In what sense, if any, are we called to battle with the Amorites? These questions are raised not only by the stories in Deuteronomy 1—3, but also at numerous points elsewhere in the book, especially chapter 7.

Within the opening chapters we can already see two quite different attitudes. On the one hand, the people related to Israel are treated with tolerance and even compassion. Like Israel, they too possess a "promised land" given by the Lord (2:5, 9, 19), indeed, won by the Lord's fighting for them just as God fights for Israel (2:21). It is almost as if we have several chosen people and several promised lands, and this close relationship reflects those traditions harking back again to a special divine blessing bestowed on the peoples deriving from Abraham and Sarah. The peaceful attitude toward Edom, Moab, and Ammon here is all the more impressive when we realize that elsewhere, even in Deuteronomy, hostility is just as likely (see Exod. 15:15; Num. 20:14–21, where Edom threatens Israel; Deut. 23:3; 2 Sam. 8:2, 12–14).

On the other hand, the benevolent attitude toward the Abrahamic peoples contrasts sharply to that directed against the "Amorites," using the term loosely for all the inhabitants of the lands promised to Israel. While Sihon and Og are represented here as initially hostile, the overture to Sihon (Deut. 2:26–29) appears as a trick in the light of *God's* initial hostile intentions (vv. 24–25); indeed Sihon's aggression is finally attributed to the Lord's doing, much like that of the pharaoh in Exodus (v. 30; see Exod. 10:20, 27;11:10). Moreover, even the aggression of the enemy cannot excuse the policy of genocide in which "men, women, and children" are annihilated, leaving "not a single survivor" (Deut. 2:34; 3:6). Later, in 7: 1–2, such a policy of complete destruction will be commanded directly by Moses, and thus implicitly by God (see 6:1).

Contemporary readers cannot help but be disturbed by such passages in the Bible. We know about atrocities throughout history perpetrated in the name of some great cause—even a religious cause. We know of Auschwitz and the "killing fields" of Cambodia and of an obscure Vietnamese village named My Lai. We know of places like Wounded Knee where Native Americans were massacred, and of El Salvador, a country named for Jesus Christ but where nuns and priests are murdered. Contemporary people of faith often want to reject any biblical passage that appears to support such immoral policies.

There are reasons, however, why these militant texts are prominent in Deuteronomy, reasons that tend at least to explain the harsh rhetoric, if not to excuse the literal meaning. We shall explore these reasons more conveniently when we come to Deuteronomy 7. But it is important now to raise the question of different modes of interpretation that extend beyond a literal reading. After all, the stories in chapters 1—3 are hardly applicable to most contemporary readers, who do not find themselves in battle with fierce giants or conscripted into rampaging armies.

For those who still want to use these stories (they are, after all, part of scripture and thus a "rule of faith"), one option has been allegorization. I once had a colleague who often quipped, "How goes the battle with the Amorites?" by whom he meant my students. He was employing an allegorical reading of Deuteronomy 1.

More seriously, we can interpret these stories as if they were like John Bunyan's famous *Pilgrim's Progress*, complete with characters and subjects reminiscent of those in the novel: the Amorite fortifications are like Doubting Castle, the Anakim are like Giant Despair, and the promised land is like Celestial City. Similarly, we could think of the enemies in the stories as forces in our lives that threaten to defeat us spiritually. As Bunyan thought of doubt and despair, we might think of a major illness, or grief, or a divorce. In fighting such forces, we may well need to muster that trust in the Lord that Israel lacked, precisely because there *are* giants there, in our lives, and their destructive power is real.

One could also include political and social powers like racism, poverty, and injustice. Such applications of the text are by no means illegitimate, nor must what is threatening always be some dark power. I have often thought that the story in Deuteronomy 1 would make an excellent text for a baccalaureate sermon ("There Are Giants There!").

Although a literal interpretation threatens to remove the text from any relevance to our lives, an allegorical (or spiritual) one can remove it from the historical roots that make it theologically compelling, if still troublesome. These stories are, after all, about the possession of land, and thus about political issues more than personal problems. It will not do to transform the land into some spiritual category divorced from historical reality. This is the danger in equating Canaan with a "celestial city" or heaven (as in the hymn "On Jordan's Stormy Banks"). The Bible in general is deeply invested in historical particularity, and that means that the spiritual realm of God is not to be found completely apart from earthly things like land, government, and economic systems.

Consider the following readers of these stories and how they might identify (or have identified) with either the character of Israel and the desire for land, or with the Amorites as victims: European settlers of "America"; Native Americans displaced to "reservations" by those settlers; disenfranchised native (i.e., black) South Africans; Russian Jews immigrating to contemporary Israel; Palestinians displaced by Russian Jews immigrating to Israel; landless peasants in Central America. One could imagine a lively, if not hostile, debate between some of these, especially since some have been considered the "Amorites" by others!

Such issues as recent as today's headlines remind us that the question of sovereignty over land is for many people a matter of life and death, just as it is in the biblical stories. It is also a matter for difficult theological reflection. A connection between land and religious faith may not be recognized within the halls of the United Nations, but it is still operative in groups as wide ranging as Native American worshipers of the Great Spirit in Montana or Christian peasants in Nicaragua. We should steer a course between a literalism in which the text means nothing to us, and a spiritualism in which the text means nothing to *others* for whom the desire for land is critical.

LAST WILL AND TESTAMENT
Deuteronomy 3:23–29

> 3:23 **At that time too, I entreated the LORD, saying:** 24 **"O LORD GOD, you have only begun to show your servant your greatness and your might; what god in heaven or on earth can perform deeds and mighty acts like yours!** 25 **Let me cross over to see the good land beyond the Jordan, that good hill country and the Lebanon."** 26 **But the LORD was angry with me on your account and would not heed me. The LORD said to me, "Enough from you! Never speak to me of this matter again!** 27 **Go up to the top of Pisgah and look around you to the west, to the north, to the south, and to the east. Look well, for you shall not cross over this Jordan.** 28 **But charge Joshua, and encourage and strengthen him, because it is he who shall cross over at the head of this people and who shall secure their possession of the land that you will see."** 29 **So we remained in the valley opposite Beth-peor.**

The opening literary unit of Deuteronomy concludes with the speaker's evocation of his own death (3:23–29), and with a sermon (4:1–40). As already announced in 1:37, God has forbidden Moses to enter the promised land "on account of" the people's rebellion. Now Moses again mentions this subject, including a report of his poignant plea for reconsideration, and the Lord's equally angry rejection. In an alternate understanding, Moses' fate is blamed on his own fault (Num. 20:1–13, reflected also in Deut. 32:48–52), but the Deuteronomists insist that the blame lies with the people (note again "on your account," 3:26). Moses suffers because of the sins of others. His death outside the promised land thus illustrates a sober theological recognition of the power of corporate evil, which can overwhelm even the innocent leader (See 2 Kings 23:24–30). Deuteronomy ends with Moses' ascent of Mount Nebo, from which he will see the promised land, but on which he will die and be buried. When Martin Luther King Jr. evoked this scene on the night before his tragic death, the relevance of Deuteronomy's portrait of a prophet fallen "on account of" the people's sin (in this case, the sin of racist hatred) was confirmed for our time.

There is also a more positive implication resulting from Moses' rejection. According to Deuteronomy, Moses learns of his fate thirty-eight years before it comes to pass (see 2:14). During the entire wilderness wandering, he remains the faithful leader of the very people whose rebellion causes his doom. Now he delivers his greatest legacy—his final testament—in the face of death outside the land. The motivation that is frequently on his lips "that you may live to enter and occupy the land, (for example, 4:1)—is one in which he cannot share. Moses thus models what faith really is: It is loyalty rooted in love, and integrity rooted in righteousness, irrespective of either reward or punishment. He thus models the human counterpart to the love of God for Israel (see 7:7–8), and deserves the title "the servant of the Lord" (34:5).

The significance of Moses' premature death, however, extends beyond a theology of corporate guilt and his own integrity. Indeed, the primary significance lies in the effect of his reminder on his audience, and how they listen to his message. In addition to 1:37–38 and 3:23–29, Moses again refers to his imminent death near the end of the following sermon (4: 21–22). The frequent repetition of his coming departure from Israel's leadership underscores the seriousness of the occasion of his speeches. The Talmud indicates that the words of a dying man are as binding as a deed which is written and delivered. The references to Moses' death show that what follows (indeed, the whole of Deuteronomy) is his last will and testament. These are his final words, and their finality makes them all the more weighty and demanding of attention.

The story in chapter 1 describes what happens when the people do *not* listen to Moses (see especially 1:26 and 43). Soon they will not be *able* to listen to him, because he will be no more. When they go into the land, he will not be with them to instruct them. They will not have Moses; they will have only his words. This is precisely the grammatical and theological connection with the sermon in chapter 4.

LIVING THE WORD
Deuteronomy 4:1–40

4:1 So now, Israel, give heed to the statutes and ordinances that I am teaching you to observe, so that you may live to enter and occupy the land that the LORD, the God of your ancestors, is giving you. 2 You must neither add anything to what I command you nor take away anything from it, but keep the commandments of the LORD your God with which I am charging you. 3 You have seen for yourselves what the LORD did with regard to the Baal of Peor—how the LORD your God destroyed from among you everyone who followed the Baal of Peor, 4 while those of you who held fast to the LORD your God are all alive today.

5 See, just as the LORD my God has charged me, I now teach you statutes and ordinances for you to observe in the land that you are about to enter and occupy. 6 You must observe them diligently, for this will show your wisdom and discernment to the peoples, who, when they hear all these statutes, will say, "Surely this great nation is a wise and discerning people!" 7 For what other great nation has a god so near to it as the LORD our God is whenever we call to him? 8 And what other great nation has statutes and ordinances as just as this entire law that I am setting before you today?

9 But take care and watch yourselves closely, so as neither to forget the things that your eyes have seen nor to let them slip from your mind all the days of your life; make them known to your children and your children's children— 10 how you once stood before the LORD your God at Horeb, when the LORD said to me, "Assemble the people for me, and I will let them hear my words, so that they may learn to fear me as long as they live on the earth, and may teach their children so"; 11 you approached and stood at the foot of the mountain while the mountain was blazing up to the very heavens, shrouded in dark clouds. 12 Then the LORD spoke to you out of the fire. You heard the sound of words but saw no form; there was only a voice. 13 He declared to you his covenant, which he charged you to observe, that is, the ten commandments; and he wrote them on two stone tablets. 14 And the LORD charged me at that time to teach you statutes and ordinances for you to observe in the land that you are about to cross into and occupy.

15 Since you saw no form when the LORD spoke to you at Horeb out of the fire, take care and watch yourselves closely, 16 so that you do not act corruptly by making an idol for yourselves, in the form of any figure—the likeness of male or female, 17 the likeness of any animal that is on the earth, the likeness of any winged bird that flies in the air, 18 the likeness of anything that creeps on the ground, the likeness of any fish that is in the water under the earth. 19 And when you look up to the heavens and see the sun, the moon, and the stars, all the host of heaven, do not be led astray and bow down to them and serve them, things that the LORD your God has allotted

to all the peoples everywhere under heaven. ²⁰ But the LORD has taken you and brought you out of the iron-smelter, out of Egypt, to become a people of his very own possession, as you are now.

²¹ The LORD was angry with me because of you, and he vowed that I should not cross the Jordan and that I should not enter the good land that the LORD your God is giving for your possession. ²² For I am going to die in this land without crossing over the Jordan, but you are going to cross over to take possession of that good land. ²³ So be careful not to forget the covenant that the LORD your God made with you, and not to make for your-selves an idol in the form of anything that the LORD your God has forbidden you. ²⁴ For the LORD your God is a devouring fire, a jealous God.

²⁵ When you have had children and children's children, and become complacent in the land, if you act corruptly by making an idol in the form of anything, thus doing what is evil in the sight of the LORD your God, and provoking him to anger, ²⁶ I call heaven and earth to witness against you today that you will soon utterly perish from the land that you are crossing the Jordan to occupy; you will not live long on it, but will be utterly de-stroyed. ²⁷ The LORD will scatter you among the peoples; only a few of you will be left among the nations where the LORD will lead you. ²⁸ There you will serve other gods made by human hands, objects of wood and stone that neither see, nor hear, nor eat, nor smell. ²⁹ From there you will seek the LORD your God, and you will find him if you search after him with all your heart and soul. ³⁰ In your distress, when all these things have happened to you in time to come, you will return to the LORD your God and heed him. ³¹ Because the LORD your God is a merciful God, he will neither abandon you nor destroy you; he will not forget the covenant with your ancestors that he swore to them.

³² For ask now about former ages, long before your own, ever since the day that God created human beings on the earth; ask from one end of heaven to the other: has anything so great as this ever happened or has its like ever been heard of? ³³ Has any people ever heard the voice of a god speaking out of a fire, as you have heard, and lived? ³⁴ Or has any god ever attempted to go and take a nation for himself from the midst of another na-tion, by trials, by signs and wonders, by war, by a mighty hand and an out-stretched arm, and by terrifying displays of power, as the LORD your God did for you in Egypt before your very eyes? ³⁵ To you it was shown so that you would acknowledge that the LORD is God; there is no other besides him. ³⁶ From heaven he made you hear his voice to discipline you. On earth he showed you his great fire, while you heard his words coming out of the fire. ³⁷ And because he loved your ancestors, he chose their descendants after them. He brought you out of Egypt with his own presence, by his great power, ³⁸ driving out before you nations greater and mightier than your-selves, to bring you in, giving you their land for a possession, as it is still to-

day. ³⁹ **So acknowledge today and take to heart that the LORD is God in heaven above and on the earth beneath; there is no other.** ⁴⁰ **Keep his statutes and his commandments, which I am commanding you today for your own well-being and that of your descendants after you, so that you may long remain in the land that the LORD your God is giving you for all time.**

(For vv. 41–43, which follow the chronology duplicated in Num. 35:6, 9–34, compare the legislation regarding homicide in Deut. 19:1–13.)

In 4:1, the connective "so now" means "therefore"—therefore, because of the stories that Moses has just retold, and because of Moses' impending death, *listening* to what he says is of the utmost importance, a matter of life and death. As if those stories were not enough, Moses immediately adds that of the infamous Baal-peor incident (v. 3; see Numbers 25). The insertion of this reference, otherwise awkward and puzzling, was perhaps prompted again by the geographical setting as well as the content of the story. Moses and his audience are encamped near Beth-peor (Deut. 3:29), roughly where they had been when the Baal-peor incident happened. Also, that incident occurred just after Israel had transversed or conquered the peoples of East Jordan, so the temporal setting is similar to that of Moses' audience as well. Finally, it is also a story about worshiping other gods, a subject directly related to the rest of the sermon. Again the implication is, remember and do not repeat!

The rest of the sermon in Deuteronomy 4 provides one of the best examples of the emphasis on word and hearing in the Judeo-Christian religions. The scope of the sermon is enormous, including references to the creation, Israel's ancestors in Genesis, the exodus, the conquest of Canaan, the exile, and even the return from exile (see 4:32–34 and 4:27–30). But the central focus of the sermon is on the giving of the covenant at Horeb (Sinai), and the implications of *how* the covenant was given—that is, by sound, not by sight. While Moses appeals to what Israel saw (4:3, 9, 11, 34, 36b), the thrust of the sermon is on what Israel heard— or, more specifically, *that* Israel heard. *What* Israel heard will be reiterated in Deuteronomy 5—the "ten words" or commandments. Here the focus is on the medium of the message: "Then the Lord spoke to you out of the fire. You heard the sound of words but saw no form; there was only a voice" (4:12). This verse is, in effect, the sermon's "text."

This sermon is also an anticipation of the Ten Commandments in Deuteronomy 5 in that it is basically an exposition of the Second Commandment, prohibiting the making of idols and the worship of other gods (5:8–10; see 4:16–19). We shall return to a discussion about the nature of religious images themselves in chapter 4, below. At issue here is the *manner* of the Lord's self-revelation and the appropriate *response* of the people. God did not appear in a *form* that could be *seen* and then *made*, or physically copied; God spoke in a *voice* that could be obeyed and followed (compare 5:27). Since God's primary self-revelation is in words, the primary form of worship is in listening, and since those words have an imperative force (especially the words of command—v. 2), the primary form of service is obedience. Indeed, Hebrew uses the expression "listen to the voice of" to mean "obey" or "heed," as in 4:30. Obedience is a peculiar form of listening—one that results in *acting* in accordance with the words that are heard.

Israel's worship, then, is an imitation of the way that *God* has related to Israel. Israel is called to hear and remember just as God hears and remembers. Israel has a God who hears whenever the people call (Deut. 4:7; see Psalms 4:3; 18:6; 20:9; etc.). Indeed, the people's very existence is rooted in this hearing, for when Israel cried out in bondage, God heard and remembered the oath to the ancestors (Exod. 2:23–24; 3:7, 9) and brought Israel out of Egypt. It is this story of exodus and covenant that demonstrates the Lord's claim to be the exclusive God for Israel (Deut. 4:34–39), and this story is the narrative basis for Israel's exclusive worship of the Lord.

That worship, therefore, is most appropriate which corresponds to this story of God's hearing and being heard (exodus and covenant). The most appropriate response to that story is not to make statues that represent the form of God, but to be a people whose life represents (that is, re-presents, makes present again and again) God's deeds—the liberation of the oppressed and the creation of a community of law and justice.

DEVOURING FIRE, UNFAILING MERCY

By the end of Moses' sermon, a tension has appeared to which I referred in the introduction, and to which I shall return in chapter 14. On the one hand, Israel's life depends on hearing God's word and living according to it. Whether the next day of the new Israel to whom Moses speaks will be D-Day or doomsday depends on what they do. This God is "a devouring fire," and disobedience will result in utter destruction (4:24, 26). On the other hand, that destruction is not complete or final, for the Lord is also "a merciful God" (4:31) who will hear Israel's repentant call (4:29) and who will again remember the covenant with the ancestors. If the primary emphasis in Moses' sermon is on the necessity of Israel's hearing the Lord, the final word (almost certainly addressed to the Babylonian exiles) is the assurance that God is forever the one who will hear *Israel's* cry, the one who will not forget.

It would be a mistake to interpret this affirmation of the grace of God as permissive, for it is invoked only after the dire consequences of Israel's irresponsibility have run their course. For the exilic author, doomsday had indeed arrived, and thus God's covenant justice had been carried out, but he also believed that the bond of God's love was stronger than the bond of God's law. As another preacher to the exiles put it, " But Zion said, 'The LORD has forsaken me, my Lord has forgotten me.' Can a woman forget her nursing child, or show no compassion for the child of her womb? Even these may forget, yet I will not forget you, . . . says the LORD" (Isa. 49:14–15, 18).

2. Covenant and Commission
Deuteronomy 4:44–5:33

At Deuteronomy 4:44 the narrator reappears, creating a second and much longer speech for Moses that continues until chapter 27 and constitutes one of the longest sermons on record. Deuteronomy 4:44–49 read like a second introduction to the book, and once may have served that purpose. It duplicates much of the information that appears in 1:1–5. Just as Moses expounded torah in Deuteronomy 1—4 (see 1:5), so now he sets torah before the people again (4:44).

RETELLING THE STORY
Deuteronomy 4:44–5:5; 5:22–33

4:44 This is the law that Moses set before the Israelites. 45 These are the decrees and the statutes and ordinances that Moses spoke to the Israelites when they had come out of Egypt, 46 beyond the Jordan in the valley opposite Beth-peor, in the land of King Sihon of the Amorites, who reigned at Heshbon, whom Moses and the Israelites defeated when they came out of Egypt. 47 They occupied his land and the land of King Og of Bashan, the two kings of the Amorites on the eastern side of the Jordan: 48 from Aroer, which is on the edge of the Wadi Arnon, as far as Mount Sirion (that is, Hermon), 49 together with all the Arabah on the east side of the Jordan as far as the Sea of the Arabah, under the slopes of Pisgah.

5:1 Moses convened all Israel, and said to them:

Hear, O Israel, the statutes and ordinances that I am addressing to you today; you shall learn them and observe them diligently. 2 The LORD our God made a covenant with us at Horeb. 3 Not with our ancestors did the LORD make this covenant, but with us, who are all of us here alive today. 4 The LORD spoke with you face to face at the mountain, out of the fire. 5 (At that time I was standing between the LORD and you to declare to you the words of the LORD; for you were afraid because of the fire and did not go up the mountain.) And he said. . . .

[The text of the Ten Commandments appears in chapters 3, 4, and 5, below.]
5:22 These words the LORD spoke with a loud voice to your whole assembly at the mountain, out of the fire, the cloud, and the thick darkness, and he added no more. He wrote them on two stone tablets, and gave them to me. 23 When you heard the voice out of the darkness, while the mountain was burning with fire, you approached me, all the heads of your tribes and your elders; 24 and you said, "Look, the LORD our God has shown us his glory and greatness, and we have heard his voice out of the fire. Today we have seen that God may speak to someone and the person may still live. 25 So now why should we die? For this great fire will consume us; if we hear the voice of the LORD our God any longer, we shall die. 26 For who is there of all flesh that has heard the voice of the living God speaking out of fire, as we have, and remained alive? 27 Go near, you yourself, and hear all that the LORD our God will say. Then tell us everything that the LORD our God tells you, and we will listen and do it."

28 The LORD heard your words when you spoke to me, and the LORD said to me: "I have heard the words of this people, which they have spoken to you; they are right in all that they have spoken. 29 If only they had such a mind as this, to fear me and to keep all my commandments always, so that it might go well with them and with their children forever! 30 Go say to them, 'Return to your tents.' 31 But you, stand here by me, and I will tell you all the commandments, the statutes and the ordinances, that you shall teach them, so that they may do them in the land that I am giving them to possess." 32 You must therefore be careful to do as the LORD your God has commanded you; you shall not turn to the right or to the left. 33 You must follow exactly the path that the LORD your God has commanded you, so that you may live, and that it may go well with you, and that you may live long in the land that you are to possess.

At first sight, one may rightly question why it is necessary to have Deuteronomy 5 at all. Why repeat the Ten Commandments here? Why not simply say, "See Exodus 20"? Moses could have slipped in such a parenthetical footnote when he referred to the "ten words" in Deuteronomy 4:13, and moved on to what is now chapter 6 (the reference to the "ten words" is reflected in an alternate designation of the Ten Commandments as the "Decalogue").

The reason for the repetition of the Decalogue is that some significant reinterpretations are incorporated into it. Just as one can see differences between the spy story in Deuteronomy 1 and its counterpart in Numbers 13—14, so here one can detect differences from Exodus 20 in the presentation of the Decalogue. Those changes are in both content and narrative framework.

The most significant differences in the content of the Ten Commandments occur in the Fourth and Tenth Commandments. The sabbath commandment begins with the imperative "observe" (Deut. 5:12) rather than
"remember" (Exod. 20:8), then moves to remembering at the end (Deut.
5:15). As a result, the ordinance of the sabbath serves the purpose of com-
memorating the community's origins. If people work all week long, they
do not have time to pause and remember the spiritual source that gave
them life. Even recreation may not produce such memory. As one minister I know said to a parishioner, "Yes, you can worship God on the golf
course, but *will* you?"

In addition, the inclusion of servants or slaves (Deut. 5:14) in the time
of rest is explicitly intentional—almost as if the law is more for them than
for the householders. Similarly, the most striking difference between
these commandments and the Exodus Decalogue occurs in the overall
motivation for obedience. There the sabbath law is rooted in the story of
creation (Exod. 20:11); here it is rooted in the exodus story (Deut. 5:15).
The law serves as an extension of that liberation from bondage. Every sabbath serves to recall the exodus, and thus every sabbath *is* a weekly exodus,
a day of freedom.

The difference in the Tenth Commandment is more subtle, and some
would say inconsequential. "Wife" appears before "house," and is the object of a different verb than what follows. It is possible that this signals a
status for the wife that sets her apart from the property of the husband's
household. The NRSV seems to suggest this possibility by presenting the
commandment in two separate paragraphs. But this interpretation is debatable, however desirable it may be.

The status of the wife illustrates the exclusively male perspective of the
commandments—there is no prohibition against coveting a neighboring
husband! Like many others, this commandment is conditioned by its time
and place, and by the socioeconomic realities of an ancient Near Eastern
culture. We will return to this and other questions about the content of
the Decalogue below.

"NOT WITH OUR ANCESTORS"

In the wider literary context of the book, the differences in terms of narrative structure are more important than differences in content. In Deuteronomy 4 the story of God's appearance at Horeb is retold to emphasize the manner of divine revelation and its consequences for the manner

of worship. Here in chapter 5 the story is retold as one of covenant making, highlighting its function as legal process.

The primary purpose of the retelling is to reconfirm the contractual relationship between the Lord and Israel, and to affirm the legitimacy of Moses as the covenant mediator. That is, the story answers the question, How did Moses get the authority to be the negotiator of the treaty between God and Israel? A negotiator cannot act unless authorized by both parties of an agreement. President Jimmy Carter could serve as the mediator of a peace treaty between modern Israel and Egypt only because both nations accepted his invitation to negotiate through him at Camp David. By what authority does Moses speak for God and for Israel? The framework to Deuteronomy 5 not only answers this question but also establishes the authority of Moses' words for the rest of the book of Deuteronomy.

Contractual agreements have various requirements in order for them to be legally binding. Getting married, buying a house, bequeathing possessions, forming a business partnership, all must be executed in a particular way if they are to be legitimate. So it was with covenants in the ancient Near East. The narrative framework to the Decalogue in Deuteronomy 5 specifies the requirements of the contract between the Lord and Israel, with the emphasis falling on the role of Moses as covenant mediator.

The covenant is with "all Israel" (5:1), a favorite phrase within Deuteronomy. In fact, 5:3 stretches grammatical felicity and historical credibility in order to emphasize that the covenant is "with us" (5:2). Moses says, "not with our ancestors did the Lord make this covenant, but with us, we, these, here, today, all of us living" (my literal translation). The sentence emphasizes the presentness of the covenant bond. In view of the tradition of the death of the exodus generation (2:16), Moses' present audience either were mere infants or were not even born when the covenant was made at Horeb. Thus 5:3 is not historically true; it is a fiction, but one of those fictions (like Jesus' parables, for example) that tell a truth of a different order than history. By including his present audience within the story of covenant making, by declaring that the "we" who stand here at the boundary of Canaan is the "you" to whom the Lord spoke "face to face at the mountain" (5:4), Moses includes the present generation as a formal party to the treaty. Moreover, the author clearly understands this process of identification to apply to *every* generation (see 29:14–15). Much as every native-born United States citizen is automatically bound by the Constitution and Bill of Rights, so every Israelite is bound by the covenant with the Lord.

There is some confusion of traditions reflected in 5:4 and 5, and it is not clear at verse 6 to whom God is speaking (compare Exod. 19:25 and 20:1). Deuteronomy wants to affirm that the entire people were at the mountain when God spoke, but also emphasizes that without Moses there to mediate God's words, they would have heard nothing. In the companion frame (5:22–27) the text seems to suggest that the people have heard the *sound* of God's words (Hebrew *qol* can mean "voice" or "sound" or even "thunder," as in Exod. 19:19), rather than the words themselves. After that, they appoint Moses to continue receiving God's revelation. They have been so frightened by the appearance of God that they are not willing to continue listening: "Go near, you yourself [emphatic use of pronoun], and hear. . . . Then tell us . . . and we will listen . . ." (Deut. 5:27). By having the tribal heads and elders make the request, the author underscores the official status of Moses' appointment. Moses is authorized as the mediator between Israel and God, and then God approves of his position as well (5:28–29). With the people departed to their tents, Moses receives "all the commandments, the statutes and the ordinances" (v. 31).

In short, the retelling of the Horeb/Sinai covenant legitimates all that Moses is now about to teach (see 4:44; 6:1; 12:1; and, at the end, 26:16). Although the covenant-making process within the whole book will not be complete until other formalities are met (mutual oath taking, witnesses, deposit of treaty document; see 26:16–19; 30:19; 31:26), the formal agents of the process are now established. The people are bound to the words of the Lord, *and* to the words of Moses. Indeed, they know the words of the Lord only through Moses, and when they say to him "hear (for us)," they are acknowledging their acceptance of Moses' authority to say to them, "Hear, O Israel" (6:4).

THE MEDIATED WORD

A long history of tradition begins here with the office of covenant mediator and continues to the present. In 18:15–22 Moses refers back to chapter 5 and reports the means whereby a replacement for him will be designated by the Lord. His successor is called a prophet, and thus serves a different function than Joshua, who replaces Moses primarily as military leader (1:38; 31:7–8, 14–15, 23). Like Moses, the prophet will mediate the word of God to Israel with authority: "him you shall heed" (literally, "listen to"). Thus the Mosaic office provides the basis for those prophets of the Lord who will follow, whose message will often begin with the words, "thus says the Lord" (see already Exod. 5:1).

The covenant mediator is also invoked in the New Testament. At Jesus' transfiguration a voice comes out of a cloud (see Exod. 19:9, 16; Deut. 4:11; 5:22) designating Jesus as God's son and says to the disciples, "listen to him" (Mark 9:7; see also the baptism story, Mark 1:11). Indeed, God is otherwise almost completely speechless in the Gospels, and it is only through Jesus that we can know God's word, just as it is with Moses in Deuteronomy. Similarly, apostolic authority is rooted in the claim to speak "the command of the Lord" (for example, Paul in 1 Cor. 14:37; note the correlation with prophecy).

The Roman Catholic tradition of *ex cathedra* pronouncements assumes a similar authority. Protestant traditions of ordination include a "horizontal call" from the congregation or other judicatory and a "vertical call" from God, a process like the dual appointment of Moses in Deuteronomy 5.

At the same time, the introduction to the Decalogue (Deut. 5:2–3) suggests that a *communal* authority is also inherent to the covenant community. Indeed, covenant community and communal authority are two sides of the same coin. The "statutes and ordinances" are to be learned by all (5:1) and taught by all, especially by parents to children (see 4:9; 6:2, 7). To be a member of a covenant people is to assent to a set of communal norms, a common core of values, that are rooted in a common heritage (expressed most concretely in a narrative—see chap. 6).

This is not to suggest that there is no room for disagreement; many people today, for example, will dispute Paul's judgment about the status of women in the church as a "command of the Lord" for our own time (1 Cor. 14:33b–38). But it does mean that an individual's spiritual experience must be balanced with the experience of the community of faith, as that experience is reflected in scripture and tradition (examples of tradition would include creeds, catechisms, official church pronouncements, authoritative customs, and generally accepted teachings). This is what it means to affirm that the covenant was not made with our ancestors "but with us, who are all of us here alive today." To be a member of the church is to interpret our own experience in the light of scripture and tradition, even though at times our interpretation may lead us to conclude that what God is saying to us today differs from what God said to Israel three thousand years ago.

HEARING THE VOICE OF GOD

What do I mean by those two apparently simple words, "God said"? The Deuteronomic emphasis on Moses as the mediator of the covenant between God and Israel, and thus as the mediator of God's word, suggests an answer to this question. The word of God is a mediated word. It comes through human words. This means that the expression "God said" is a metaphor. For at least a hundred years, most biblical scholarship has operated with the conviction that the words "God said" should not be taken literally. The expression does not mean that a supernatural being having the physical organs of mouth, tongue, vocal chords, and lungs actually spoke Hebrew words out of the sky, and that people (in this case, Moses) heard the words, just as they would hear the words of another human being. Instead, most biblical scholars prefer to think of these words as metaphorical. A metaphor is a word or expression that literally denotes one thing but is used in place of another to suggest a likeness between them. The transfer of senses fits only in a poetic, figurative way. To take the expression literally ruins the effect.

Consider, for example, a famous line from Carl Sandburg: "The fog comes / on little cat feet." That is a wonderful metaphorical description of fog. The poet provides a rich field of meaning by associating an animal's movement with a meteorological phenomenon. In other words, Sandburg has given us an imaginative picture that enables us to grasp something about this elusive substance called fog. He turned fog into a catlike being in order to help us understand something about it. But it would be ridiculous to turn the metaphor into a literal description, to think that fog really has feet with fur and claws. It would also be foolish, however, to assume that Sandburg's metaphor has not given us something essentially true about fog. In fact, the poet's symbolic language tells us something that objective, direct description cannot. Consider a dictionary definition of fog: "condensed water vapor in cloudlike masses close to the ground and limiting visibility." That may be effective as a weather forecast, but it cannot evoke in us a sense of the *presence* of fog, and thus it has none of the power of Sandburg's metaphor.

What the poet did with fog, the biblical authors did with God. Of course, describing God is far more complicated than describing fog. But scholars are increasingly recognizing that the language of theology is closer to the language of poetry (generally understood) than it is to the language of straight, objective reporting. The biblical authors recognized that God is not an object that we can describe in the same way that we can describe a chair or a mountain or a tree. Hence they used many metaphors to describe God—a rock, a female eagle, a soldier, a woman in the throes of childbirth. But one metaphor dominates—God is pictured as a human being who acts and speaks. Just as our modern poet chose the most appropriate animal to talk about fog, so the biblical authors chose the most appropriate animal to talk about God—the human animal.

The Ten Commandments are human words about God, about what God wants for human society. Thus these words, including the phrase "God said," are part of the metaphorical picture of God. To take these words literally, as an exact report of an audible voice, would be to misinterpret them. It would be to turn poetic language into objective, descriptive language. It would be like saying that fog really has feet. At the same time, we must also say that to dismiss the Ten Commandments as merely human words, with no transcendent dimension, is to fail to understand the depth of their meaning and significance. That is the secularist fallacy. It is like saying that fog is always only "condensed water vapor." If, for many people in the twentieth century, the Bible has become unintelligible, it is perhaps not so much because of a lack of belief as a failure of the imagination. While literalism is intellectually unappealing, secularism is spiritually unsatisfying.

Thus the Deuteronomic emphasis on Moses as the mediator of the words of God points to a larger theological truth: All words about God are mediated words, words that come to us through the human community. This is why many theologians resist the dangerous equation of the Bible with the "word of God" and insist that the Bible is a *witness* to the word of God. It can *become* the word of God only when the Spirit speaks through the written words, that is, the human words of scripture.

Those words are much like the temple built by Solomon, about which he says: "The Lord has said that he would dwell in thick darkness. I have built you an exalted house, a place for you to dwell in forever. . . . But will God indeed dwell on the earth? Even heaven and the highest heaven cannot contain you, much less this house that I have built!" (1 Kings 8:12–13, 27). Indeed, this passage, probably deriving from the Deuteronomic school, uses the same metaphor of "thick darkness" as Deuteronomy 5:22 to suggest that God is ultimately inscrutable and therefore cannot be "contained," even by words. This is a subject to which we shall return in discussing the meaning of the Second Commandment.

3. The First Commandment
Deuteronomy 5:6–7; 6:1–25

The Ten Commandments are the heart of biblical law. Most of us probably think of law as something that exists by itself. Law is a collection of rules. Rules are simply prescriptions or prohibitions of behavior: Do this, don't do that. They may also contain a sanction: If you do this, then you will pay with that. Thus law is a straightforward list of rules with associated punishments for breaking the rules.

If one asked the author of Deuteronomy if this understanding of law is correct, he would say, "It is only half right." Law *is* a collection of rules, and a good portion of Deuteronomy is such a collection. But, the author would say, there is something more fundamental to law than the rules themselves, as important as they are. This other half of the law is not rules but a story. If one jumps straight to the rules, without understanding the story in which the rules are embedded, then one is likely to misunderstand the rules themselves. The rule of law derives from the ruling metaphor that governs one's life.

The Ten Commandments do not begin with a command to do this or not do that. They begin in Deuteronomy 5:6 with the summary of a story: "I am the LORD your God, who brought you out of the land of Egypt, out of the house of slavery." This is a summary of the first half of the book of Exodus, the story of the people's liberation from the political oppression of Pharaoh. The covenant community into which they are now called is rooted in that story. The laws that follow are rooted in that story. The story of the exodus is the "root metaphor" from which all of the law grows; without that story, the law itself would wither and die, just as a tree will wither and die when cut off from its roots.

THE GRAND CENTRAL STORY
Deuteronomy 5:6–7

> 5:6 **I am the LORD your God, who brought you out of the land of Egypt, out of the house of slavery;** [7] **you shall have no other gods before me.**

In some way, every person has a "grand central story." In using this expression I evoke the picture of the train station in New York City—Grand Central Station. Here all rail lines seem to converge. Just so, each of us has one central story that serves as the focal point for all others, ultimately determining our values and beliefs, the way we live and the way we die.

The great power of all stories resides in their ability to be both enticing and transforming. Stories entice us by drawing us into another world. We immediately sense this attraction as soon as we read the classic opening line, "Once upon a time there was. . . ." We hardly need hear the next words before we are already there, in the story, and the "was" becomes "is" in our imagination. The story does not simply give us information or new facts; it gives us new horizons, new perspectives, new responsibilities.

We enter the world of the story even more deeply when we imaginatively identify with the characters, whether they be in *Little Women, Hamlet,* or the parable of the prodigal son. In that process of imaginative participation in the world of the story, we become one of the actors.

If the story is unusually powerful, we emerge from its world not simply entertained but transformed, our identity changed, our life reshaped by the story's shape, our perception of the everyday world altered by the "story-shaped world." In a word, we are captivated by the story. Authoritative stories are the ones that we come back to, over and over again, because they have the power to change who we are and how we live.

"I am the LORD your God, who brought you out of the land of Egypt, out of the house of slavery." This is the story of ancient Israel's origin, the narrative that shapes the community's identity, Israel's "grand central story." This narrative reveals to them the central truth about life, and it is remembered and repeated from one generation to another. It is not first the law that determines who we are and how we shall live; it is the story that undergirds the law. For, as critic Amos Wilder has noted, "It takes a good story to make people realize what the right thing to do is. The road to moral judgment is by way of the imagination" (Wilder, *Rhetoric,* 1964, 60).

Thus the story that most captures our imagination is the beginning of the law. That is why the sentence, "I am the LORD your God, who brought you out of the land of Egypt, out of the house of slavery," stands at the beginning of the Ten Commandments. This was the story that most captured ancient Israel's imagination. From one generation to another, this was the story that Israel told and retold.

"WE WERE PHARAOH'S SLAVES"
Deuteronomy 6:1–9, 20–25

6:1 Now this is the commandment—the statutes and the ordinances—that the LORD your God charged me to teach you to observe in the land that you are about to cross into and occupy, 2 so that you and your children and your children's children, may fear the LORD your God all the days of your life, and keep all his decrees and his commandments that I am commanding you, so that your days may be long. 3 Hear therefore, O Israel, and observe them diligently, so that it may go well with you, and so that you may multiply greatly in a land flowing with milk and honey, as the LORD, the God of your ancestors, has promised you.

4 Hear, O Israel: The LORD is our God, the LORD alone. 5 You shall love the LORD your God with all your heart, and with all your soul, and with all your might. 6 Keep these words that I am commanding you today in your heart. 7 Recite them to your children and talk about them when you are at home and when you are away, when you lie down and when you rise. 8 Bind them as a sign on your hand, fix them as an emblem on your forehead, 9 and write them on the doorposts of your house and on your gates.

[For a discussion of 6:10–19, see chapter 8, below.]

6:20 When your children ask you in time to come, "What is the meaning of the decrees and the statutes and the ordinances that the LORD our God has commanded you?" 21 then you shall say to your children, "We were Pharaoh's slaves in Egypt, but the LORD brought us out of Egypt with a mighty hand. 22 The LORD displayed before our eyes great and awesome signs and wonders against Egypt, against Pharaoh and all his household. 23 He brought us out from there in order to bring us in, to give us the land that he promised on oath to our ancestors. 24 Then the LORD commanded us to observe all these statutes, to fear the LORD our God, for our lasting good, so as to keep us alive, as is now the case. 25 If we diligently observe this entire commandment before the LORD our God, as he has commanded us, we will be in the right."

When the Israelite child asks, "What is the meaning of the decrees and the statutes and the ordinances that the Lord your God has commanded you?" the parent is instructed to answer by retelling the story of the exodus: "We were Pharaoh's slaves in Egypt. . . ." The child is asking for no less than the ground of all ethical behavior, the spiritual and moral character of the community called Israel. The answer does not lie in the law itself, even though the content of the law may well be beneficial. The answer also does not lie in authoritarianism ("because God said so").

Rather, the answer lies in the narrative that defines both divine and human identity, that reveals both the character of the Lord and the character of Israel. The meaning of the law is found in the narrative, and the narrative (if one genuinely responds to it) leads to the *responsibility* of the law. The connection between who we are (identity) and how we behave (responsibility) results in "righteousness" (6:25). Righteousness is being in right relationship with God, who is the primary subject of the narrative, and being in that relationship means at the same time to live justly.

The parent is to say "*we* were Pharaoh's slave in Egypt" to emphasize the crucial importance of identifying with that story. That is why the introduction to the Ten Commandments in Deuteronomy 5:3 deliberately distorts historical fact in order to encourage spiritual participation by every subsequent generation. Only by an imaginative participation in the story is it *their* story.

The Passover liturgy of Judaism illustrates the importance of this identification. It quotes the question from Deuteronomy 6:20 approvingly, saying that wise children ask the question this way. Then it cites a similar question from Exodus 12:26 ("What do *you* mean by this observance?") and criticizes children who implicitly exclude themselves from the people's story, saying that if they had been there at the original exodus they would not have been redeemed!

"I am the LORD your God, who brought you out of the land of Egypt." In Judaism this verse alone is the first of the Ten Commandments (Deut. 5:7–10 form the second). It does not sound like a commandment. It is not a "do this" or "don't do that." But it is recognized as a commandment, and the *first* commandment, because the story that most captivates our imagination provides the foundation for all that we will do or not do. Because the story *captivates* our imagination, it also has the power to *command* what we shall be. The story has an imperative force just as powerful as the explicit commandments that follow.

Sometimes when parents want to correct misbehavior in children, they say, "That's not the way you were brought up." That is a narrative form of discipline. It is saying, "Your behavior should be based not simply on rules but on a story—the personal narrative of your upbringing—and your behavior should be consistent with that narrative." The preface to the Ten Commandments (according to the Protestant reading) translates this principle into a communal context: "I am the LORD your God, who brought you out of the land of Egypt, out of the house of slavery." This story defines the way the Hebrews were "brought up" (quite literally) and thus determines their character.

So it is with us, we who stand far removed from the time of the story. It is imagination that provides access to this story over time. It is imagination that allows us to participate in the story, to become part of the story, to be addressed by the story. When we hear the story addressing us, we are hearing the voice of God. When the story "speaks to me," as we say, then God is speaking. When the "you" of the story becomes "me," God is at work through my imagination, determining who I shall be, and commanding how I shall live.

We live in a time marked by increasing lawlessness, perhaps because we have no grand central story to undergird the way we live. Perhaps crime prevention needs to start with story provision. That, at least, is where the Ten Commandments start, and where Moses recommends that each family start, in retelling the story that provides the community's identity.

"I am the LORD your God, who brought you out of the land of Egypt, out of the house of slavery." To hear myself included within that "you" is the beginning of faith. It is also the beginning of the law. The most important question for any of us is this: What story will so captivate our imagination that it will command the way we shall live? Will it be the Christian story (which includes the exodus), or some other story? What we imagine determines who we are and what we do. How do we imagine ourselves? How do we imagine our community? Our world?

There once lived a people whose imagination was captivated by a story that opened up a new world, a world where people were freed from oppression, brought into a new relationship with God and with each other—a covenant community—and offered the way to become God's realm of peace and justice on earth. This was a people with a vivid imagination! Let us hope that ours is no less grand.

THE GOD OF GODS

"I am the Lord your God, who brought you out of the land of Egypt, out of the house of slavery." Ancient Israel's identity was rooted in this story of liberation, of being set free from bondage to Pharaoh. But the story of the exodus is only half the story that shapes Israel's identity. The other half begins with the formation of the covenant community and the gift of the Ten Commandments.

The pharaoh from whom Israel was freed was considered by the Egyptians as himself a god, and the living representative of all the gods of Egypt. Israel was freed from Pharaoh in order to be free for the Lord.

Throughout the exodus story, the Lord gave an order to Pharaoh, "Let my people go, that they may serve *me*." Throughout the Bible, there is no "freedom from" without a "freedom for." In other words, there is no absolute freedom from serving some god. The question is, *which* God will you serve?

The First Commandment (5:7 according to Reformed numberings) leaves no ambiguity about whom Israel *should* serve: "You shall have no other gods before me." The grand central story leads to the great commandment, as it has become known in both Jewish and Christian tradition (see Matt. 22:36). This commandment is not only first in order but first in importance, as subsequent portions of Deuteronomy insist repeatedly.

Yet the meaning of this commandment is not nearly as simple as it may seem. A literal translation would be: "Nor shall there be for you other gods before my face." The last phrase is the most difficult. Because the word "face" often stands for the word "me," the phrase could mean "beside me," or "before me," or, more loosely, "to my disadvantage." Most likely, it means "in front of me" or "before me," perhaps originally referring to placing idols in God's presence. The Lord's exclusive royalty will not allow for any rivals. When the Queen of England passes by, no loyal subject would dare to stand and stare into her face without first bowing. Just so, another god may not stand before the Lord, because the Lord is the God of gods.

Thus we can already see that something about this commandment does not fit with much popular understanding. The commandment is not a theological statement of monotheism. It does not say that there is only one god. It does not claim or even suggest that "other gods" do not exist or are not real. Contrast the central affirmation of Islam: "There is no God but Allah." Our commandment does not say, "There is no God but the Lord." It says, to Israel, and thus to us: "*You* shall not have other gods on a level equal to me." Relatively late in Israel's history, the prophet known as Second Isaiah did claim that there was no God but the Lord, and that all the other gods were nothing (Isa. 41:21–24; compare Deut. 4:35, 39, probably from an exilic editor); but for most of Israel's preexilic history, the reality of divine beings other than the Lord was not explicitly questioned.

The Old Testament speaks clearly about other gods who exist. As Psalm 82:1 says, "God has taken his place in the divine council; in the midst of the gods he holds judgment." The beginning of the book of Job describes a similar scene, when the "heavenly beings came to present themselves before the Lord" (1:6). Or consider the vision of the prophet Micaiah, who "saw the Lord sitting on his throne, and all the host of heaven standing beside him on his right hand and on his left" (1 Kings 22:19; see Deut. 33:1). These passages portray the heavenly court as an assembly of gods.

There were also, of course, the gods of other peoples, gods with names like Moloch, Marduk, Asherah, Astarte, and Baal. It is possible that even these gods were thought to be in the Lord's court. At least one ancient text tells of the God of Israel, called the "Most High," assigning a god to each of the nations (Deut. 32:8; see 33:27).

But the Old Testament leaves no question about the hierarchy of divine beings. It was ruled by the Lord, the God of gods (indeed, this expression is used in Deut. 10:17). As Psalm 89:6–7 puts it, "Who among the heavenly beings is like the Lord, a God feared in the council of the holy ones, great and awesome above all that are around him?" Psalm 82 ends with the Lord condemning the other gods to death, because they have become unjust. If the ancient Hebrews acknowledged the existence of other gods, they would be what we might call *political* polytheists, rather than *philosophical* polytheists. They were nevertheless more interested in divine power, rather than divine being. Today we are often preoccupied with the philosophical question, Does God exist? They were preoccupied with the political question, Which God is in charge?

"You shall have no other gods before me." The First Commandment is not a call to believe in the existence of only one God; it is a command to obey only one God as the God of gods. Perhaps if we insert the word "power" for "God" it will help us to understand this sentence: "You shall have no other power before me." The commandment does not claim that there is only one power; the world is full of competing powers. The question is, Which power is supreme—for *you?* "Not shall there be *for you* a power higher than God." The First Commandment does not demand belief in one God; it demands *loyalty* to one God *above all others.*

PLEDGING ALLEGIANCE

The political meaning of the First Commandment stands behind the exposition of this commandment in Deuteronomy 6, just as the preface to the First Commandment (5:6) is there reflected in the retelling of the exodus story (6:10–15). The center of Deuteronomy 6 is verses 4–5, the text that is called the "Shema" in Judaism, for whom it still functions as a central creed (*shema* is the imperative form of the verb that means "to hear"; see my discussion, above, on 5:22–27). The best translation, which incorporates not only the NRSV translation but also my own and that of S. Dean McBride, Jr., is probably the following: "Hear, O Israel: The Lord is our God, the Lord alone, so love the Lord your God with all your heart, and all your life, indeed with all your capacity."

The treaty model that I mentioned previously suggests why the translation "the Lord alone" is preferable to another traditional translation, "the Lord is one." The ancient Near Eastern treaties outlined the conditions under which the Great King's benevolent protection would continue, and the major condition was loyalty to the Great King. The Shema restates the central claim of the treaty between the Lord and Israel. The command is an expression of political theology. It demands allegiance to one power among others; it does not state that there *is* only one power. The Shema does not call for belief in monotheism; it calls for fidelity to a particular God.

The treaty context also qualifies the meaning of the word "love." Ancient Near Eastern vassal treaties used words for "love" to describe the relationship between the vassal king and the Great King. While the Hebrew word here may include some of the emotional nuances of the English word, its primary meaning again has to do with loyalty, commitment, and responsibility. This is why it is part of the *command*—that is, grammatically the imperative force of the opening word "hear" continues with the second clause, "so love."

Thus the "great commandment" is political in the sense that it forces us to choose which power we will make the highest power in our lives. Like Joshua at Shechem, it demands, "choose this day whom you will serve"—either the Lord, or some other god (Josh. 24:15). This meaning is perennially relevant because our lives are full of powers competing for our loyalty, demanding our allegiance.

Pledging our highest allegiance to God alone often creates conflicts. In the late 1940s, a public school student who was a Jehovah's Witness refused to put his hand over his heart when saying the pledge of allegiance to the flag. The child's parents had taught him that his highest loyalty was to God, and that the gesture of putting the hand over the heart symbolized giving one's highest loyalty to the state. The school officials attempted to force the student to conform, the child refused, and the case ultimately went to the Supreme Court, which decided in favor of the child. The parents of this child may well have had the Shema in mind—"love the Lord your God with all your heart"; their position is theologically in line with the command.

When we understand the First Commandment in terms of competing powers, instead of competing gods, we can see why it not only is relevant to our own lives but also raises one of the most important questions that we have to answer: What is the greatest power in our lives? Few if any of us can honestly say that God is always that power. All too often some other power takes the place of God. It may be money, or success, or status. It may be what our peers say. It may be some compulsion, some craving, some desire. It may be family, or country, or race. Whatever it is, when we place some other power "before God," we allow it to be the God of gods.

One man spoke of this problem in his own life: "I was operating as if a certain value was of the utmost importance to me. . . . I was extremely success-oriented, to the point where everything would be sacrificed for the job, the career, the company" (Bellah and others, *Habits of the Heart*, 1985, 5). This man's work had become a power that held him in bondage. That is why we need to hear this First Commandment. This commandment makes us free *for* giving ourselves not to a pharaoh who will enslave but to a redeemer who will save. "You shall have no other gods before me." This commandment is life to those who will hear and obey.

4. The Second Commandment
Deuteronomy 5:8–9a; 7:1–26

IMAGES AND THE UNIMAGINABLE
Deuteronomy 5:8–9a

5:8 **You shall not make for yourself an idol, whether in the form of anything that is in heaven above, or that is on the earth beneath, or that is in the water under the earth.** 9 **You shall not bow down to them or worship them. . . .**

(For a discussion of 5:9b–10, see chapter 14, pages 150–151.)

The Second Commandment originally prohibited the making of a carved image, or "idol", but it came to include virtually any "form" or shape. In subsequent tradition, this text became the basis for one of the most fundamental aspects of Western religions, the emphasis on auditory as opposed to visual representations of God. In Judaism, Christianity, and Islam God is primarily (and for some, exclusively) revealed through words, not through pictures; through hearing, not through seeing. Jews, Christians, and Muslims are each a "people of the book"—the Hebrew Bible, the Old and New Testaments, and the Koran. For them listening to the "word of God" is the center of the spiritual life. The architectural focus on pulpit and lectern in many churches shows how central the spoken word is to our faith, a result of the Second Commandment: You shall have no visual images of God!

The law against physical images, therefore, came from a positive affirmation. We communicate what we know about God, says ancient Israel, primarily through language, through words. Our knowledge of God is shaped first and foremost by linguistic forms, chief among them being story, but also others: laws (such as the Ten Commandments), poems, and proverbs.

But there is also a negative side to the ban on images, because, for ancient Israel, all physical images were what we think of as "idols." One dictionary defines the word "idol" as "an image used as an object of worship."

That is what the Old Testament thinks of all physical images, and numerous passages make fun of such worship (for example, 1 Sam. 5; Isa.
40:18–20; 44:9–20; 46:1–2). Physical images of gods were available at virtually every Canaanite market, but Israelites were forbidden to wear them,
buy them, or make them. Yet the construction of such an image almost
brought about the people's death at the very foot of Horeb/Sinai (Deut.
9:6–10:11).

Ancient Israel's view of images almost certainly represented a misun-
derstanding of their proper function. From what we know of other ancient
Near Eastern peoples, they did not naïvely think that the physical images
of their gods were literally and exclusively *identical* to their gods. They believed that their gods were cosmic powers, not mere things of wood or
stone. The object of their worship was not the "idol," say, of the Babylonian god Marduk, but the god Marduk himself. It would be better to describe an idol as "an *object* used as a *means* of worship." The idol was simply a visual representation of the god that served to guide the faithful in
their devotion. Of course, it is easy for superstition to turn the image into
something more, to invest the full being and power of the god in the physical image, but that is a distortion of the image, not its intended role.

Such superstition regarding images is caricatured in the modern folk
song that says, "I don't care if it rains or freezes, 'long as I got my plastic
Jesus, sittin' on the dashboard of my car." The same could be said for statues of the Buddha. No Buddhist in his right mind would claim that the
Buddha *is* the mound of sculptured rock with a human form, only that the
statue helps to focus the devotee's thinking into *right* thinking, thereby
opening up one of the "Four Noble Truths."

The positive affirmation in the Second Commandment will always be
true of Christian faith—language will always remain the primary means
to our knowledge of God. But the negative side points to something
deeper than the use of physical images. It points to the negation of all images that attempt to represent the mystery of God, including linguistic images. A sad irony has been our inability to see the potential idolatry not
only in visual images of God but in word images. After all, the very commandment that prohibits physical representations of God is using a *verbal*
image of God as king, or sovereign, or lord. It is likely that such an image
may be necessary if we are to think of God as the God of gods, as the First
Commandment claims. But that image may not be sufficient in opening
up other dimensions of the nature of God.

Some years ago theologian J. B. Phillips wrote a book called *Your God
Is Too Small.* His point was that many of us grew up with particular no-

tions about God, but our notions did not grow up along with us. So we became adults with childish images of God, images that we could not accept. But in one sense *all* images of God are "too small." One of the classic philosophical definitions of God is "that than which nothing greater can be conceived." Our images of God—both in language and in visual media—are expressions of our conceptions of God. But God is not identical to those expressions. God is greater than any "form" we may use to describe God, whether the form is a word or story or law or prophetic oracle—or a painting or statue. The very name "God" is an image that we use to point to ultimate reality, but it is not identical with that reality.

In other words, there is a "God beyond 'God.' " There is something greater than that which our word "God" attempts to name. As theologian Gordon Kaufman puts it, "the real God always transcends and escapes our grasp; whenever we suppose that God has become directly available to us or is in some way (even intellectually) disposable by us, we can be certain it is an idol with which we have to do and not God" (Kaufman, *Essay*, 49).

A Zen Buddhist would probably smile and say, "Of course. God is not God! Recognizing that is necessary for enlightenment." "God" is not God. If we fail to recognize the truth in this apparently paradoxical negation, we risk trivializing the mystery that is the real God, and thus keeping an image of God in our minds that is "too small." One of the great Christian mystics, Meister Eckhart, said, "No image has ever reached into the soul's foundation, where God herself, with her own being is effective." (If Eckhart's reference to God as feminine upsets you it may be because your image of God as exclusively male is also "too small"!) And Thomas Aquinas said, "Then alone do we know God truly, when we believe that God is far beyond all that we can possibly think of God."

Does this mean that we must give up using word images for God? Of course not. We can no more stop using language to describe God than we can stop using it to give shape to all our experiences. But we must recognize that, even as we use images, we are imaging an unimaginable, naming the unnameable, giving a form to the one who is essentially formless. This principle stands behind what I said earlier about the "word of God" and "words of God" or "words about God," and how the expression "God said" must be understood metaphorically (see pages 46–48).

If we understand the Second Commandment as prohibiting the attempt to "grasp" God or to make God "directly available" to us, to use the theologian's phrases, then we may be free to reconsider the role of visual media in worship. Of course, the *primary* form of worship will always be that combination of remembering, hearing, and acting to which the sermon on the Second Commandment in Deuteronomy 4 refers (see above, pages 37–38). And it is difficult to envision a picture or other graphic representation *of God* as even a means to worship, although one might appeal to Michelangelo's famous painting of the creation on the Cistine Chapel ceiling.

But worship in the sense of *liturgical* actions may also include the use of visual arts. Paintings, sculpture, dance, pantomime, and other visual media can serve as powerful expressions of personal spirituality in public worship and in various learning experiences. In fact, visual stimuli often reach us at conceptual and spiritual dimensions different from those of words. The Eastern Orthodox church has long used icons—paintings of the face of Jesus, or of Mary, or of a saint—as aids in worship. These traditions have recognized that the incarnation provides a warrant for the use of visual images that separates Christianity from both Judaism and Islam. For, as Colossians says, "Christ is the visible likeness [Greek *eikon*] of the invisible God" (1:15; see John 1:1, 14; Phil. 2:6–7; 2 Cor. 3:18). At the same time, the incarnation extends and deepens that orientation of Deuteronomy 4 to see the most appropriate expression of worship exemplified in a human life. It is in the words and deeds of Jesus of Nazareth that we come closest to a representation of what God wants for humankind.

KEEPING APART FROM THE JONESES
Deuteronomy 7:1–26

> 7:1 When the LORD our God brings you into the land that you are about to enter and occupy, and he clears away many nations before you—the Hittites, the Girgashites, the Amorites, the Canaanites, the Perizzites, the Hivites, and the Jebusites, seven nations mightier and more numerous than you—[2] and when the LORD your God gives them over to you and you defeat them, then you must utterly destroy them. Make no covenant with them and show them no mercy. [3] Do not intermarry with them, giving your daughters to their sons or taking their daughters for your sons, [4] for that would turn away your children from following me, to serve other gods. Then the anger of the LORD would be kindled against you, and he would destroy you quickly. [5] But this is how you must deal with them: break down their altars, smash their pillars, hew down their sacred poles, and burn their idols with fire. [6] For you are a people holy to the LORD your God; the LORD your God has chosen you out of all the peoples on earth to be his people, his treasured possession.
>
> [7] It was not because you were more numerous than any other people that the LORD set his heart on you and chose you—for you were the fewest

of all peoples. ⁸ It was because the LORD loved you and kept the oath that he swore to your ancestors, that the LORD has brought you out with a mighty hand, and redeemed you from the house of slavery, from the hand of Pharaoh king of Egypt. ⁹ Know therefore that the LORD your God is God, the faithful God who maintains covenant loyalty with those who love him and keep his commandments, to a thousand generations, ¹⁰ and who repays in their own person those who reject him. He does not delay but repays in their own person those who reject him. ¹¹ Therefore, observe diligently the commandment—the statutes, and the ordinances—that I am commanding you today.

¹² If you heed these ordinances, by diligently observing them, the LORD your God will maintain with you the covenant loyalty that he swore to your ancestors; ¹³ he will love you, bless you, and multiply you; he will bless the fruit of your womb and the fruit of your ground, your grain and your wine and your oil, the increase of your cattle and the issue of your flock, in the land that he swore to your ancestors to give you. ¹⁴ You shall be the most blessed of peoples, with neither sterility nor barrenness among you or your livestock. ¹⁵ The LORD will turn away from you every illness; all the dread diseases of Egypt that you experienced, he will not inflict on you, but he will lay them on all who hate you. ¹⁶ You shall devour all the peoples that the LORD your God is giving over to you, showing them no pity; you shall not serve their gods, for that would be a snare to you.

¹⁷ If you say to yourself, "These nations are more numerous than I; how can I dispossess them?" ¹⁸ do not be afraid of them. Just remember what the LORD your God did to Pharaoh and to all Egypt, ¹⁹ the great trials that your eyes saw, the signs and wonders, the mighty hand and the outstretched arm by which the LORD your God brought you out. The LORD your God will do the same to all the peoples of whom you are afraid. ²⁰ Moreover, the LORD your God will send the pestilence against them, until even the survivors and the fugitives are destroyed. ²¹ Have no dread of them, for the LORD your God, who is present with you, is a great and awesome God. ²² The LORD your God will clear away these nations before you little by little; you will not be able to make a quick end of them, otherwise the wild animals would become too numerous for you. ²³ But the LORD your God will give them over to you, and throw them into great panic, until they are destroyed. ²⁴ He will hand their kings over to you and you shall blot out their name from under heaven; no one will be able to stand against you, until you have destroyed them. ²⁵ The images of their gods you shall burn with fire. Do not covet the silver or the gold that is on them and take it for yourself, because you could be ensnared by it; for it is abhorrent to the LORD your God. ²⁶ Do not bring an abhorrent thing into your house, or you will be set apart for destruction like it. You must utterly detest and abhor it, for it is set apart for destruction.

Moses would not be a good choice for the speaker at an interfaith banquet. If readers of Deuteronomy have not already perceived Moses' shortcomings in the area of pluralistic acceptance while reading chapter 1, they will surely see it in reading chapter 7. I include chapter 7 along with a discussion of the Second Commandment because it is an extension of the prohibition of images and of worshiping other gods (the First Commandment). The first two commandments themselves are closely linked in that the reference to "them" in Deuteronomy 5:9 refers back not to the "idol" (singular) of verse 8 but to the "other gods" of verse 7. Chapter 7 is a passionate (some might say fanatic) sermon on the first two commandments played out in terms of the imminent conquest of Palestine that confronts Moses' audience.

Deuteronomy 7 is essentially a sermon about religion and culture and about what it means to be an Israelite instead of a Canaanite. The sermon is particularly relevant for Moses' audience, which is headed for Canaan, but it is also applicable to anyone who wants to live an authentic faith in the midst of a culture that may not share that faith, or even offers radically different alternatives to it.

To ask about our place in culture is to ask where we belong. The word "belong" meant originally "to be thoroughly suited," and it is related to the root for "to yearn, long for." To what are we "thoroughly suited"? For what do we fervently yearn? These are deeply religious questions. They are also central to the Judeo-Christian faith, and the way we answer them indicates whether we are genuinely Christian.

If we turn to the metaphorical language of the Bible, we can reduce these questions to one: How do I relate to "the world"? By "the world," the biblical authors meant not simply the physical earth but also the culture in which they lived. Culture includes virtually everything that has to do with being human, from language to habits, institutions, government, art, values, and so on. If you were an ancient Israelite asking Moses about Canaanite culture—the culture of the promised land—you would have received an unmistakably clear answer: The culture of Canaan, the land to which you are headed, is evil, and you shall have no part of it. In fact, you shall utterly destroy it.

There are probably few passages in the Bible that most of us find more distasteful than portions of Deuteronomy 7. Moses portrays the imminent conquest of the land of Canaan as a process that would include the all-too-familiar atrocities of war. God will "clear away" all the nations who live there. Once Israel has defeated them, even "survivors and fugitives" will be destroyed (v. 20). The Israelite conquerors must not subvert God's intentions by making peace treaties with the Canaanites, nor by allowing their young people to marry Canaanites. When the conquerors come upon Canaanite worship places, with their various images, they must destroy them as well (7:5, 25–26). The entire process of "search and destroy" falls under a technical military term of "holy war," namely, "the ban" (Hebrew *ḥerem*, 7:2, 26—"utterly destroy," "set apart for destruction"; compare the warfare legislation in chapter 20, especially verses 10–18, which at best allows for the enslavement of peaceful natives).

We might contrast the attitude toward culture here with the familiar expression "keeping up with the Joneses." What Moses recommends is not simply "keeping apart from the Joneses"; rather, it is getting rid of the Joneses in order to remove the temptations of "the world." Canaanite culture is a threat to faith, and thus to life itself. Again the treaty model suggests why matters of faith are life-and-death concerns. If a vassal king entered into treaty relationships with rulers other than the Great King, he committed breach of contract and would be punished severely. If such illicit treaties involved actions of outright treason (for instance, joining in military operations against the Great King), the vassal's state would be invaded and the vassal king executed, along with many of his people. Just so, Deuteronomy reasons, if Israel makes covenants with the Canaanite peoples, it is a breach of the covenant with the Lord. This breach would be all the more serious because making covenants usually involved invoking the deities of both parties, and thus recognizing the authority of the deities as equal, something that would be inconsistent with the First Commandment. In short, religious apostasy was equivalent to political treason, and would have correspondingly dire consequences.

Before we leap to the conclusion that this rejection of culture is peculiar to the *Old* Testament, let us remember that it appears in the New Testament as well. Listen to this admonition that Jesus gives his disciples in the Gospel of John: "If the world hates you, be aware that it hated me before it hated you. If you belonged to the world, the world would love you as its own. Because you do not belong to the world, but I have chosen you out of the world—therefore the world hates you" (15:18–19). Here and elsewhere the New Testament at times reflects a self-understanding of the Christian community that we call the "sect" type. A sect sees itself as an elect group whose purity sets it apart from the surrounding culture. Most of us probably find at least the Deuteronomic version of sectarianism to be nothing short of fanatic. We live in an age when pluralism is at least allowed, if not applauded. We may work side by side with people of other faiths, a phenomenon that is only increasing as more people adopt religious traditions from the East, or more vague spiritual configurations broadly labeled "New Age."

Much of Deuteronomy 7 represents a self-righteous intolerance of other people's views. We identify the same intolerance in our own society among fanatics who seek to ban (note that word!) literary classics from public schools because they contain subjects that may not fit with the fanatics' religious views (for example, *The Wizard of Oz* because it has a witch, as well as a wizard). One group even burned *The Living Bible* on the grounds that it departs too far from the King James Version. We read about God ordering the Israelites to kill Canaanites and we think of irrational distortions of religion in pathological killers, like the man who stabbed several people to death with a sword because, he claimed, God told him to do so. When we look at religions today, we see the same frightening phenomenon magnified—for example, in some forms of fundamentalism.

Before we reject Deuteronomy 7 as a tract for fanatic religious terrorists, however, several qualifications are in order. First, it is clear from numerous Old Testament texts that Israelites perceived the Canaanites to have social and religious customs that were highly objectionable: sacred prostitution (23:17–18), child sacrifice (18:9–10), various forms of incest (see Lev. 18). For generations (from the time of Joshua until the time of Saul), the Israelites existed without a formal monarchy, and thus without many of the power structures and economic excesses that went along with Canaanite political systems (see Deut. 17:14–17). Indeed, some Old Testament scholars argue that the Israelite "conquest" of Canaan was more like a peasant revolution against the oppressive regimes of an entrenched elite. More generally, the prophets amply attest to situations in which conforming to Canaanite culture entailed abandonment of the covenant and its requirements of social justice (for example, Amos 2:4–8; 4:1–3; 5:10; 6:1–7). Thus, far more is at stake in the sermon of Deuteronomy 7 than religious ideas.

Second, while a literal reading of Deuteronomy 7 would produce a brutal religious extremism, the picture of the anticipated conquest is largely fictional. The author knew quite well that Moses' orders for the conquest were never carried out. The Israelites did not slaughter the whole population; rather, they willingly allowed their children to marry Canaanites and they even more willingly trotted off to worship at Canaanite temples. Far from keeping apart from the Joneses, the Israelites often joined them, so much so that it was often difficult to tell the difference between the average Canaanite and the average Israelite. This, at least, was the view of the entire Deuteronomic school, and it is reflected clearly in the books that follow Deuteronomy (see Josh. 6:25 and 7:10–26, and contrast Deut. 7:15b–26; Josh. 9:3–27 and contrast Deut. 7:2b; Judg. 2:11–16). Indeed, Deuteronomy 4:3–4 already refers to such an incident that happened *before* entering the land (see the related covenant prohibitions in Exod. 23:23–33; 34:11–17).

Third, much of Deuteronomy appears to reflect the apostasy of the later kings, as well as the corresponding reforms of others. Beginning with Solomon, various kings of Judah and, later, northern Israel married foreign wives, largely to establish diplomatic relations, and enshrined their respective religious traditions, including images of other gods, sometimes in the very temple of the Lord (1 Kings 11:1–13). By far the worst, again according to the Deuteronomic historian, was Manasseh (about 685 B.C.E.), whose list of heretical credentials presents striking parallels to those prohibited in Deuteronomy 7 (see 2 Kings 21:1–9). In contrast, two kings are singled out as paragons of virtue for their reforms, which destroyed such innovations. Again, the reforms are reported in terms reflecting Deuteronomy 7 (Hezekiah, about 715 B.C.E., 2 Kings 18:4–9; and Josiah, about 640 B.C.E., 2 Kings 23:4–14).

Although it is difficult to determine exactly when Deuteronomy 7 was written, it was almost certainly after at least some of these developments. If we assume a relatively early date for this chapter (for example, during the time of Hezekiah's reform), it mirrors the warning of its fictional setting; if we assume a later date (for instance, after the time of Josiah, or even after the fall of Judah to the Babylonians), it becomes a retrospective theological explanation of disaster.

"A PEOPLE HOLY TO THE LORD"

In the end, therefore, Deuteronomy 7 appears to be the condemnation of a long process of compromises with cultural values alien to the covenant traditions of Israel. The texts portray this process beginning even before the entrance into Canaan, and extending up to the fall of Judah. Although the compromises were many, nowhere are they portrayed more succinctly than in the people's request for a king, "so that we also may be like other nations" (1 Sam. 8:20).

But Israel was not called to be like every other people—they were called to be different: "for you are a people holy to the LORD your God; the LORD your God has chosen you out of all the peoples on earth to be his people, his treasured possession," (Deut. 7:6). Israel as the chosen people has a mission within the world. It is through them that God intends to model God's blessing for all humankind (Gen. 12:1–3; Exod. 19:5–6). As the covenant community, they are the showcase of divine love and justice. When other peoples look to Israel, they are to see a community that lives life to its fullest in accordance with the will of God. This is why Israel must, in some important ways, keep apart from the Joneses.

"Holiness" means "separate from, different, distinct, unusual." Israel's holiness is not inherent, not a quality that they possess by nature; it is a character derived from God's selection—they are "holy *to the Lord.*" It is only because God has called them and separated them from other peoples that they are "separate" and holy. And the reason that underlies all of this, Moses says, is that the Lord loved Israel for no other reason than that the Lord wanted to love them. It is this unconditional love that stands behind the oath to the ancestors in Genesis, and the imminent fulfillment of that oath in the people's occupation of the land of promise (7:8).

Yet again, Israel's election out of God's unconditional love is not an excuse for becoming like the other peoples. To continue in God's grace, Israel must now meet the conditions of the covenant (7:9–16; on vv. 9b–10, see the discussion of the blessings and curses in chaps. 27—28). Failure to do so would be a form of corporate suicide in which the very destruction here inflicted on the Canaanites would be turned against God's own people (7:4). The danger of self-righteous nationalism, always inherent in the claim to being God's chosen group, here meets its limit: Being God's special people entails special responsibilities, and failing to meet them entails special punishment. Divine election always has divine rejection as its potential counterpart. Here the prophetic background of Deuteronomy is evident (see Amos 3:2).

Once we put aside the exaggerated militaristic metaphors of *getting rid* of the Joneses, we would do well to listen to the warnings about *keeping up* with the Joneses. The church does not have to adopt all the characteristics of a sectarian group in order to maintain its calling as the people of God. Following in the covenant tradition, 1 Peter sees the Christian community as "a holy nation, God's own people" (1 Pet. 2:9). We too have a mission—to proclaim and to model to all the world God's redeeming love that has been revealed in the person of Jesus Christ. In order to fulfill that mission, at some point the Christian community itself has to keep apart from the Joneses. Indeed, Paul's letters to the Corinthians and Ephesians and Romans are full of discussions about how to be a Christian and *not* be an ordinary Corinthian or Ephesian or Roman.

We have something to learn from 1 Peter and Deuteronomy. We have something to learn from religious communities like the Mennonites and the Quakers. We have something to learn from the so-called sects. As Robert Bellah and coauthors write,

> the unwillingness of the sects to compromise with the world has on occasion made them marginal or even irresponsible. But the sectarian insistence on purity has an enormous contribution to make, particularly in calling [other religious communities] to examine the nature of their compromises and to try to discern when they are strategic retreats and when they are betrayals of what must not be betrayed. (*Habits of the Heart*, 1985, 247)

If we do not in some ways see ourselves as aliens within the culture that we live in (1 Pet. 2:11), then we may wonder if we are being the faithful people of God.

What is our culture? It is the quantity and quality of television we and our children watch, what movies we enjoy, and what concerts we attend. It is what books we read, what food we eat—and when and where and with whom. It is how much money we spend on clothes and a house and a car and a host of consumer goods. It is whether we spend more money on malls or schools. It is what kind of toys our children play with. It is what we do on Sunday morning and Saturday night. It is what kind of work we do and how we go about doing it, and what kinds of work we reward handsomely, and what kinds poorly. It is how we spend our vacations (notice that word "spend"). It is how we view various minorities, whether of gender, religion, race, or sexual orientation. It is that incredibly varied and fluid matrix in which we live our lives. If, in this matrix, we are not at some point considered "weird" because of our religious tradition and how we live according to that tradition, then maybe we have become too much like the Joneses.

The writer G. K. Chesterton once said that "tolerance is the virtue of people who do not believe anything." The most prominent word for the church in the New Testament is *ekklesia*, which means "called out." As the church we are "called out" of the world, not to escape from its problems but to be "set apart" from its values when they are inconsistent with the gospel. The only way that we can serve the world—also part of our calling—is if we remain a "holy people." The only way truly to represent God's kingdom *to* the Joneses is to keep apart *from* the Joneses. "Do not be conformed to this world," writes Paul to the Romans, "but be transformed by the renewal of your minds, so that you may discern what is the will of God—what is good and acceptable and perfect" (12:2).

5. The Third through the Tenth Commandments
Deuteronomy 5:11–21

MAINTAINING GOD'S REPUTATION
Deuteronomy 5:11

> 5:11 **You shall not make wrongful use of the name of the LORD your God, for the LORD will not acquit anyone who misuses his name.**

Most people probably think that using profanity—or, more simply, cursing—is what this commandment is all about. Using the word "goddamn" (notice, please, the quotation marks) is then the most severe example of breaking the commandment. Some Jewish traditions will not even allow people to *speak* what we think was God's personal name ("Yahweh"), and instead say "Adonai" ("the LORD"—as in the NRSV), or even just "the name."

Sometimes cursing can be sinful in a deeply harmful way, especially when it is directed maliciously at another person. But limiting the meaning of this commandment to cursing is a good example of moralism. Moralism takes a wrong that is relatively unimportant compared to others and elevates it to higher, or even supreme, importance. During the Watergate crisis, one prominent evangelist publicly expressed dismay on learning from the publicized White House tapes that the president had actually cursed. Here was an incident in American history in which a president deliberately lied to the public and encouraged others to do so; in which a president used his power to thwart the pursuit of justice, thereby creating a constitutional crisis of the first order. Yet what the preacher regretted was that the president took the Lord's name in vain. That is moralism.

The commandment says literally, "You shall not lift up the name of the Lord your God for emptiness." The word "emptiness" means that which is lacking in substance, worthless, hollow, trivial. Some alternate translations are: "You shall not use the name of the Lord your God trivially."

"Don't take God's name lightly." "Don't invoke God's name cheaply." Jacob did this when he lied to his father in the process of cheating his brother out of the family inheritance. When he came to his father bearing cooked domestic meat in place of the wild game that Isaac had asked of Esau, Isaac was surprised that the boy had hardly left the room before returning. So he asked him, "How did you manage to find game so quickly?" And Jacob, pretending to be the hunter Esau, said, "Because the LORD your God granted me success" (Gen. 27:1–29).

Our culture is full of people who use God's name trivially or cheaply, yet would not dare curse, at least in public. Politicians invoke the deity in campaign speeches, sometimes calculating that such an invocation will gain them votes. Some government officials appeal to loyalty to God and country to justify arming terrorists who kill nuns and children in Central America. Some televangelists trivialize the name of God with saccharine prayers and shameless appeals for money from gullible elderly men and women living on Social Security. I once received a packet of materials in the mail that included a return postcard on which I could check the box asking the evangelist to "pray for me to receive a continuous money blessing." The front of the envelope had these words: "Dear Jesus, protect this letter of help and please dear Lord let it reach this home safely we pray," as if Jesus works for the U. S. Postal Service. Sometimes the very prayer that ends "in the name of Jesus" profanes that name. A prayer can be the worst form of profanity.

"Christian" schools that were organized to avoid racial integration in public schools used God's name cheaply. Appeals to the Bible in order to deny equal rights to women use God's name cheaply. Parents who present their infants for baptism and promise to bring them up in the church use God's name cheaply if the next time they appear in church with a child is when the child is getting married. People who join the church and promise to be faithful members use the name cheaply if they drop out after two or three months. Often, our breaking of the third commandment comes after using God's name with good intentions but poor follow-through.

Consider this commandment as protection of God's reputation. The flip side would be, "lift up God's name for honor." Everyone's reputation is determined to some degree by the people with whom he or she associates. One can get a good or bad reputation just by being seen with a particular group of people. The same is true of God. God is known in the world by the people who invoke God's name, whether explicitly or implicitly. What would God appear to be like if all that you knew about God came from the Ku Klux Klan?

It is not just in our formal invocations that we can lift up God's name either to worthlessness or to honor. It is also in our everyday lives. If people identify us as Christians, then the way we live is an unspoken invocation of God's name. Friends may know us for months or years without knowing that we attend a church. But sooner or later something we say will tip them off. They may even get bold enough to say—casually, of course—"I'm sort of interested in finding a church that I would like—where do you go?" When this happens, a connection has been made. That person has looked at you, at the way you live. She knows something about your values, about your personal integrity, about your concern for particular issues. And now she has realized that you (you—of all people!) are a Christian. And that person has thought, "If that's what a Christian is like, then maybe I can be one after all. If that's what a Christian community is like, then I want to be part of it."

Paul says that Christians are "ambassadors for Christ" (2 Cor. 5:20). Ambassadors are official representatives of one government to another. Ambassadors speak and act *for* their government, out of the authority granted them *by* their government. What they say and do determines how their government is perceived, whether for good or for ill. God is a "Prime Minister" whose ministry can be accomplished only through all the "little ministers" in the world. We are called to represent God's government—which the Bible calls the realm of God—to another—which the Bible calls the world. God's reputation depends on the integrity of our speech and our actions. God is known through what we say and do. How we live determines whether God's name is cheapened or honored.

BIBLICAL "R AND R"
Deuteronomy 5:12–15

> 5:12 **Observe the sabbath day and keep it holy, as the LORD your God commanded you. 13 Six days you shall labor and do all your work. 14 But the seventh day is a sabbath to the LORD your God; you shall not do any work— you, or your son or your daughter, or your male or female slave, or your ox or your donkey, or any of your livestock, or the resident alien in your towns, so that your male and female slave may rest as well as you. 15 Remember that you were a slave in the land of Egypt, and the LORD your God brought you out from there with a mighty hand and an outstretched arm; therefore the LORD your God commanded you to keep the sabbath day.**

"What are you doing this weekend?" The fourth of the Ten Commandments suggests that our answer to this familiar question will reveal the spiritual character of our lives. This is the first commandment that begins with a positive order, rather than a "you-shall-not." It is a commandment that provides a bridge from strictly theological concerns to social concerns, because it involves our relationship not only to God but also to other members of the community. How we "spend the weekend" (to use that curious phrase), moreover, how we incorporate "sabbath time" into the rest of our week, determines the physical and spiritual health of ourselves and our community.

"Observe the sabbath day and keep it holy." What does that mean—"to keep it holy"? The root meaning of the word "holy" is "apart, separate, distinct, special," as we have seen in our discussion of Deuteronomy 7:6. Just as Israel is a people set apart, so the sabbath is a *time* set apart, distinct, special. To adapt a contemporary phrase, it is spiritual "quality time." Those for whom the word "holy" has negative connotations can think of sabbath time as "special" time. Thus we could translate the commandment, "Observe the sabbath, to make it special." *The* sabbath, of course, refers to a particular day. But "sabbath" itself refers to a quality of time that can be adopted any day of the week. This extended meaning of sabbath is particularly important in a culture, such as ours, where the sabbath day may not be the best occasion for some people to have sabbath time.

How then is sabbath time good for us? The meaning of the word "sabbath" itself provides the basic answer. The word means to stop, to cease, to desist, to rest. Sabbath time is time in which we rest from whatever activities qualify as work for us. A culture steeped in the "Protestant work ethic" has produced a work *ontology*—that is, a notion that, at the very ground of our being, we are valued for what we do (or have done) in our work. Our self-esteem derives from what we have accomplished.

There is nothing wrong with this work ethic, as such; in fact, it is a stimulus for many of our cultural achievements. But when work becomes the only source for self-esteem, or far transcends all other sources, then it threatens to distort who we are as human beings. Then work becomes a kind of addiction. It is not coincidental that our culture has coined the term "workaholic." The sabbath commandment's call for rest is a protection from the excessive demands of work, and, for some of us, the excessive *fulfillment* of work.

Sabbath time is what we call "R and R" (rest and recreation). But what qualifies as work and as rest or recreation will differ from one person to another. The same activity may be work for one person and recreation for another. Painting may be a meaningful sabbath activity for a business executive, but not for a professional landscape artist. Golf may be a good way for a physician to unwind on the weekend, but not for a golf pro on the tour. Cooking may be a refreshing adventure for a computer programmer, but not for a chef—and not, for that matter, for the one who cooks every night at home during the week. Rest from work does not require inactivity. We can do many things that are spiritually restful, *if* those activities are not already work for us. It is possible to be "at rest" while busy.

But I must make an immediate qualification. Americans are notorious for turning recreation itself into work. The purpose of playing becomes something beyond the sheer enjoyment of the activity itself. Play becomes a means to accomplishment and achievement. Thus the weekend golfer can spend hours on the driving range "working" on those iron shots. Almost anything that otherwise might easily qualify as a sabbath time activity can be turned into work: gardening, sports, the arts, music, crossword puzzles. Even spiritual development can be turned into work! It is quite possible, for example, to put so much effort into learning how to meditate that one cannot meditate. If meditation becomes something that one wants to perform skillfully, it is no longer meditation.

The original intent of the sabbath commandment appears to have been the provision of rest and recreation. We could summarize the commandment with two positive prescriptions: stop, play. Notice that the commandment does not say, "Observe the sabbath day by going to church." Indeed, in early Israelite culture, as far as we can tell, public worship attendance was only three times a year, and that only for males (Exod. 23:14–17). We rarely hear sermons on this text! It was not until later, during and after the time of the Babylonian exile, that some sort of weekly worship service came to be part of sabbath observance. The reasons for that development are complex, but basically they have to do with the situation of the Jewish communities scattered throughout the Near East, and much later, of course, throughout Europe. These communities were increasingly isolated within a pagan, or Christian, or Muslim culture. In short, regular sabbath worship came to be the way of remembering their spiritual heritage and so maintaining their communal identity.

We can observe sabbath by not working and by various forms of recreation. But sabbath time is also a time for remembering the spiritual heritage of the community of faith, and that remembering happens best in the context of public worship. In Deuteronomy, observance of the sabbath day leads to remembering the grand central story, "I am the Lord your God, who brought you out of the land of Egypt." R and R now becomes "rest and *remember*—remember that you are a child of God, remember that you are part of the people of God. Remember who is your God of gods, who is your Power of powers.

Within the Judeo-Christian tradition, rest and recreation are necessary parts of sabbath time, but they are not sufficient. One must also remember the story that contains the very commandment of the sabbath. Moreover, the *purpose* of the observance is to constitute a society in which those who are literally bound by work (servants, Deut. 5:14) may also benefit from rest. Thus the sabbath is an institution of social justice as well as of personal spirituality.

HONOR YOUR PARENTS
Deuteronomy 5:16

> 5:16 **Honor your father and your mother, as the LORD your God commanded you, so that your days may be long and that it may go well with you in the land that the LORD your God is giving you.**

Most of us probably think that the commandment to honor one's parents was intended primarily for children. "Honor" means "obey" and the commandment becomes a useful tool for getting children to do what we say. But the word "honor" does not mean "obey." Basically, it means to "show respect for," and even "to revere" (especially when God is the object). It means to ascribe to people the honor that is due to them because of who they are and how they act. Also, the Ten Commandments were not addressed to children; they were (and are) addressed to adults. This commandment thus speaks to adult children about parents, making it even more relevant for our day than it was three thousand years ago.

We are confronting issues involving aging parents that Moses and his epoch would never have imagined: the costs of health care; the need for adult day-care facilities, retirement homes, and nursing homes; the ability of modern medicine to prolong life (sometimes to prolong it beyond what seems qualitatively worthwhile); devastating diseases like Alzheimer's; and decisions about everything from whether someone is too old to drive a car to whether someone should be kept alive by artificial means. As parents grow older and more feeble, these are decisions in which their adult children increasingly will have to participate, and sometimes the children will have to make these decisions for the parents.

In the midst of all the physical care that aging parents may require, we do well to remember that spiritual care is a task of equal, and sometimes greater, significance. That is, the honoring of parents, and being honored by adult children, can be a journey of deepening relationships. This journey is often not easy, because the parenting that the parents provided may not have been completely honorable. Many children grow up with unresolved grievances, incompletely healed emotional wounds, and damaged self-esteem. They are often not even aware of these problems until they become adults themselves. Thus forgiveness and reconciliation are perhaps the most important dimensions of spiritual growth in honoring one's parents, and repentance may well be required for *both* generations. Honoring one's parents may involve the honest sharing of anger as well as affection, grudges as well as gratitude. But precisely in that sharing may also come healing, self-discovery, reconciliation, and love.

"YOU SHALL NOT MURDER"
Deuteronomy 5:17

5:17 **You shall not murder.**

Probably none of the Ten Commandments is quoted more frequently and for such different causes than the sixth, traditionally translated: "you shall not kill." Almost every week we see a picture of a protester carrying a sign inscribed with these words, but the protest can be against capital punishment, abortion, war, or euthanasia. Some people think that executing a man who brutally raped and murdered a child is a form of killing not much higher than the crime. Some people think that terminating the life of an embryonic fetus is a form of killing similar to that done by the criminal. Some people think that withholding antibiotics from a ninety-five-year-old person in a persistent vegetative state is killing.

But in each of these cases other people—often equally spiritual or religious—will argue that these actions resulting in death can be right and good, depending on the circumstances. People who invoke the Sixth Commandment on one issue are often incensed when others invoke it on another issue. One can imagine a scene in which two groups, each carrying signs saying "thou shall not kill," end up using their signs to beat each other to death!

As in other languages, Hebrew has several words for killing. The word that is used here occurs far less than others. More importantly, the word has a limited range of meaning and use. It never refers to killing in warfare. It would not be fitting for accidental death, for death from disease, or for suicide. Thus many forms of killing are *not* automatically included within the original denotations of this word.

Nevertheless, the use of the word is not entirely consistent. It is occasionally used for capital punishment (Num. 35:30) and for unintentional or accidental killing of one person by another (as in Deut. 4:41–42; 19:1–7). Yet the Sixth Commandment almost certainly does not include these exceptions, for capital punishment is often called for in Old Testament law and it is not logical to prohibit accidental killing.

To what form of killing, then, does the prohibition refer? Most interpreters agree that it refers to murder, as several contemporary translations put it: "you shall not murder." Murder made it into the short list of Ten Commandments because it is a threat not only to individual life but to the life of the community. A society that permits murder is *not* a community but a mob of barbarians. Since we live in a society that, in 1990, committed 25,000 murders, many of them with handguns, we might sometimes wonder if we are disintegrating into such a mob.

The question now becomes, What constitutes murder? To answer that question, first from a biblical perspective, we have to go outside the Ten Commandments. Numbers 35:16–21 offers a different law from the Sixth Commandment. This law is lengthy and detailed. It is not an absolute prohibition but a circumstantial definition. It does not begin with the imperative words "do not" but with the conditional word "if." It states the circumstances under which the act of killing can be called "murder." Those circumstances include the type of object used, whether the act was planned ahead of time, and if the act was done with malice. In other words, the intent and motivation behind an act help to determine whether it is murder. In particular, the act is murderous if done out of personal "hatred" or "enmity" (Num. 35:20 and Deut. 19:11, using the same Hebrew word; in general, compare Deut. 19:1–13).

The Sixth Commandment and the law in Numbers represent two different types of law. Scholars refer to them as absolute law and case law. Absolute laws tend to be black and white, with no ifs, ands, or buts. For example, "whoever strikes father or mother shall be put to death" (Exod. 21:15). Case law tends to make the ifs, ands, or buts crucial to the determination of fault, as well as punishment. For example, compare another situation involving "striking" someone in Exodus 21:18–19. In each law, the action—striking a person—is the same, but in one it is punishable by death, and in the other, only by a financial payment, at most.

The biblical tradition holds together absolute and case law. On the one hand, it lays out some forms of behavior (such as murder) that are absolutely intolerable in a civilized society; on the other hand, it recognizes that the morality of many actions depends on the circumstances in which they are done, on the motivations behind the actions, and on the consequences that follow. In a loose sense, absolute laws affirm that a society cannot exist without basic rules, while case laws affirm that "rules are made to be broken" (or at least more carefully defined).

The limited range of the Hebrew word in question means that contemporary use of the Sixth Commandment by itself to oppose many forms of killing is unwarranted. Whether one opposes abortion or war, euthanasia or capital punishment, an appeal to the Sixth Commandment is an appeal to a prohibition that will not, on its own, support such opposition. In considering the questions of life and death that increasingly force themselves on us, we would do well to follow the biblical precedent.

Modern medical technology alone has placed within our hands the ability to control life and death to a degree that our biblical ancestors would have found unimaginable. As a result, we are confronted with ethical decisions of enormous complexity and equal gravity. But we must also recognize that, precisely because of the complexity of these decisions, we cannot formulate laws that will determine what is right and what is wrong for every situation. Reality is too complicated for that.

It is interesting that there is no law code in the New Testament similar to the law codes in the Old Testament. Unlike Moses (and, later Muhammad), Jesus is not portrayed in the Gospels as a new lawgiver. Consider Jesus' only recorded commentary on the Sixth Commandment: "You have heard that it was said to those of ancient times, 'You shall not murder'; and 'whoever murders shall be liable to judgment.' But I say to you that if you are angry with a brother or sister [without cause] you will be liable to judgment" (Matt. 5:21–22). Jesus does not issue a new law on what does or does not constitute murder. He is interested instead in condemning the *personal attitude* that can lead to murder, the attitude that is the opposite of love, namely, hatred. His saying is conventional in that it reflects the underlying *motivation* of murder singled out in the Old Testament texts; his saying is radical because it could apply to virtually anyone. That is, virtually everyone is angry with someone at some time. Perhaps it was to narrow application that some ancient textual authorities use the term "without due cause" in conjunction with anger.

There is, of course, a place for law. It is essential for social order and for justice. But the *gospel* is not law; it is love. That is why Paul could say that "the commandments," including the sixth, "are summed up in this word, 'love your neighbor as yourself.' " Love does no wrong to a neighbor;

therefore, love is the fulfilling of the law" (Rom. 13:8–10). And the way that love works in every situation cannot be predetermined by law.

ADULTERY
Deuteronomy 5:18

> 5:18 **Neither shall you commit adultery.**

Americans always seem to have a mixture of reactions to adultery. On the one hand, it is the subject of jokes that make light of the matter. On the other hand, it is often elevated to the top of the sin list. In the first case its personal and social injury is underestimated; in the second it is inflated by moralism—that is, exaggeration (see the discussion above, on the Third Commandment, page 71). The latter is especially prominent in political election years, when a candidate's marital infidelity is often treated as more important than his or her position on the economy, unemployment, environmental crises, and nuclear war.

When we hear the word "adultery" we probably think about the actions of two people. The biblical authors thought instead of how the actions of two people affect the entire social fabric. The prohibition against adultery made it to the list of top ten principles because adultery posed a threat to that fabric. Adultery is prohibited because it is a breach of *a social institution*, marriage, not because it may be emotionally harmful to the offended spouse. This focus on the welfare of the community is often at odds with the focus of our contemporary culture. How many people, contemplating an affair, will stop to think, "How will this affect the society in which I live?"

But before we move too quickly to adopt the biblical view of adultery, we need to look more carefully at what it includes (and excludes), and especially how it affected women. In the Old Testament adultery is not simply an offense against one's spouse. Adultery is also an offense of one *man* against another. Male adultery is limited to having sex with another man's wife or fiancée, whether or not the offender is married. Thus a married man who had sex with an unmarried woman, even with a prostitute, was not committing adultery. A married woman who had sex with an unmarried man committed adultery against her husband. The sexism inherent in the biblical laws on adultery involves a double standard. Similarly, men were allowed to have multiple wives, and also concubines, but women were not allowed to have multiple husbands, and certainly not male concubines (for King David, see 2 Samuel 3:2–5; 5:13–16).

Whether the double standard in marriage customs included the assumption that wives were the property of their husbands is debatable. For example, the commandment on coveting in Exodus seems to include the wife along with the husband's other material possessions, that is, along with "anything that belongs to your neighbor" (Exod. 20:17). Some scholars think that the Deuteronomic version separates the wife from the property, thus recognizing her status as an individual (Deut. 5:21; note also the two different verbs, "covet" and "desire"). But another text can associate a man's possessions (house, vineyard) with his wife (Deut. 20:5–7). Still, even slaves were not considered property in the sense that one could do anything with them, and certainly wives were no less protected by law (compare Deut. 21:10–17; 22:13–21).

Despite the ambiguous status of women in terms of property, it is nevertheless clear that they did not enjoy equal sexual freedom with men. As a result, the commandment on adultery reflects social attitudes that most of us would find unacceptable. For us, adultery can no longer be seen only as an offense against the *husband* of a marital relationship, nor can we exclude affairs between married men and unmarried women. For us, adultery means a married person having sex with anyone other than his or her spouse. But is this broad definition sufficient? Is it, in fact, broad enough?

Consider Jesus' saying about divorce in Matthew 5:27–28: "You have heard that it was said, 'You shall not commit adultery.' But I say to you that everyone who looks at a woman with lust has already committed adultery with her in his heart" (Matt. 5:27–28). A male Sunday school teacher I know chose this saying of Jesus to begin a course on troublesome Bible passages. When he read it to the class, one of the men stood up and said, "Time to go home!" Apparently Jesus' extension of the commandment made him uncomfortable. Jesus says that whoever even thinks about having sex with someone other than his spouse is committing adultery. Even Jesus, open as he was to women in ways unusual for his time, still seems to be thinking only of *male* adultery. But we will assume that for us this saying applies to both men and women.

What is the significance of Jesus' extension of the commandment? It is similar to the way he extended the prohibition of murder to include malicious anger. Jesus is interested not in formulating a new law, but in going to the heart of the old law. Adultery is not limited to sexual actions but includes the mental inclination to engage in those actions. The actions are simply the completion of a thought. By radicalizing the commandment, Jesus has, in a sense, *relativized* the importance of the actions. Adultery is committed before any act is done.

The point of this, of course, is not to say that the physical act itself is insignificant. Nor should we take the saying to imply that, since we have thought about it, we might as well go ahead and do it. Rather, the point is to emphasize that the real problem in adultery is infidelity—that is, unfaithfulness. Adultery is first a breach of trust between two people, and (especially considering the marriage vows) a breach of promise. Adultery is a spiritual reality before it is a physical act. It begins in the soul long before it moves to the bedroom. Indeed, infidelity may never lead to the bedroom, or even have sexual overtones, if we follow Jesus' lead in extending the meaning of the term.

Sometimes adultery is simply a symptom of an attitude toward sexuality that seems amoral, if not immoral. We use the phrase "casual sex" to refer to people who engage in sexual acts as if the emotional and institutional bonds of a monagamous relationship are insignificant. At other times, the emotional break occurs first, and adultery begins with alienation or estrangement between two people who were previously intimate, connected, integrated, and whole. This alienation is what we mean by the word "sin." Sin is separation of what was previously together, as well as the sexual act that may result from that separation. Almost always, alienation between two people is not the "fault" of only one but of both in interaction with each other. Adultery as a physical act is simply a symptom of adultery as infidelity, and of the prior alienation. In a way, alienation is *more* profound in casual sex because it is, by definition, sex without relationship in any meaningful sense.

The extension of the meaning of adultery beyond the reference to a sexual act is most important if we are to attempt to answer the question, Is adultery always wrong? The question itself is peculiarly modern, and, some would say, already a sign of a collapse of values. But as we have seen, adultery is a culturally relative term. We consider some acts adulterous that some biblical texts do not condemn. In our country, polygamy is illegal, while in others it is the norm—and even sanctioned by religion. So what we call adultery may be, in some other culture, simply a different form of marriage. Some situational ethicists would say that adultery is wrong only if someone is emotionally hurt. So-called open marriages are supposed to allow for more than one sexual partner if both spouses agree. Whether such situations are possible, however, given human nature, is highly questionable. Where monogamy is the custom, it would be an exceedingly rare situation in which sexual relations outside marriage could happen without hurting someone and without being a manifestation of alienation, infidelity, and estrangement.

If, then, we understand adultery as infidelity resulting from alienation between two people, we are understanding it as sin. But that is not the final word that the Christian tradition has to offer. When Jesus was confronted with a woman caught in adultery (John 8:3–11), he said to her (male) accusers, "Let anyone among you who is without sin be the first to throw a stone at her." The accusers quietly drifted away, one by one, "beginning," the text says, in an interesting detail, "with the elders." The longer one lives, the more one knows how deeply alienation is part of one's *own* past, and the more one can say, "this easily could have happened to me." And one can bet that these men had at least on some occasion looked at another woman with lust in their heart, and so, according to Jesus' teaching, had also committed adultery.

When the men are all gone Jesus addresses the woman, asking her, "Woman, where are they? Has no one condemned you?" She answers, "No one, Lord." And Jesus says, "Neither do I condemn you; go, and do not sin again." Jesus neither condemns nor condones. His response is neither punitive nor permissive. Jesus does not repeat a doctrine; he responds to a person. He does not offer a new law; he offers love. He offers forgiveness but also a challenge—a charge, really—to begin life anew.

We need a healthy balance of the two: the severity of the law, which warns us of the dangers of infidelity and the harm that it can do to others, but also the lenience of love, which recognizes the complexity and fallibility of all human relationships, and, in compassionate humility, in the end judges not, that it be not judged.

LIVING IN A DEN OF THIEVES
Deuteronomy 5:19

5:19 Neither shall you steal.

Few of us probably feel smitten when we hear the Eighth Commandment, "You shall not steal." We think of stealing as something done by thugs in dark alleys, or professional criminals who rob banks, or perhaps someone who breaks into a house looking for money for the next cocaine high. The commandment may originally have referred to a special type of stealing, namely, kidnapping for the purpose of selling the victim to someone else for use as a slave (see Exod. 21:16; Deut. 23:7). This practice was not uncommon in the ancient Near East. Recall the story of Joseph, who was captured (not without the help of his jealous brothers) and sold into slavery in Egypt (Genesis 37). In fact, such kidnapping is still not uncommon in parts of the contemporary Far East, much as it was part of American history from the sixteenth through the mid-nineteenth century.

But before we discard the Eighth Commandment as irrelevant to our own behavior, let's look more closely at its intent. Stealing for the purpose of selling into slavery was particularly reprehensible to the ancient Hebrews precisely because it *was* part of their communal history—they came from an enslaved people. Such stealing is a denial of the fundamental human right of personal freedom and dignity. Such stealing robs people not merely of their material possessions but of their status as an independent person, created in the image of God. Thus the fundamental basis of the biblical prohibition of stealing has to do with the *personal* worth of every human being.

Thus we can already see that biblical law imposes limitations on an economic (that is, commercial) activity for a theological reason. But the Eighth Commandment seems to go further. Because of its very brevity, it does not specify kidnapping alone, but seems to prohibit all forms of stealing; and, if we look elsewhere in the Old Testament, we find this to be the case. Biblical law extends beyond the stealing of people to the stealing of people's *property*, say an ox or a sheep (Exod. 22:1).

The most serious aspect of stealing is not the consequent deprivation of property but the denial of the personal dignity of the victim. That denial happens even when the victim is unaware of the crime. After all, stealing comes in many forms, some direct (as in a mugging), some indirect (as in embezzlement). Biblical law is aware of both. If one looks beyond explicit references to stealing, one will find numerous laws prohibiting various actions that, in effect, constitute stealing. For example, some laws prohibit the possession of false weights and measures used to charge unfair prices for agricultural products (Deut. 25:13–16), and one law prohibits the secret moving of boundary markers to enlarge one's land (19:14). Both of these actions would result in stealing, even though the victim probably would not even know what had happened.

Direct and indirect forms of stealing also exist in our own culture. The indirect forms are particularly common in what is called "white-collar" crime. People who would never dream of mugging someone and taking their wallet think nothing of cheating on their income tax, embezzling funds at the office, or asking their thirteen-year-old child to say she is twelve at the theater ticket window. Students who would not think of taking a jacket from someone's locker think nothing of taking answers from another's exam paper. A man who would not think of stealing a car thinks nothing of hiding serious defects in his car when he sells it. Yet all of these are forms of stealing.

Our culture fails to understand something about stealing that is implicit in the context of the Eighth Commandment: the prohibition is part of a *social* ethic, not a merely individual one. Thus the law prohibits particular actions that, while not strictly theft, would result in the denial of some people's basic needs. For example, the "gleaning law" prohibits farmers from harvesting their entire crops for themselves. They are not allowed to harvest a field to its very border, but must leave a strip of crops around the perimeter for the benefit of the poor. They are also not allowed to go over the crops a second time to gather the "leftovers." They are for the poor also. If farmers harvest all their fields entirely, they are taking from the poor. In effect, they are stealing (Deut. 24:19–22).

There is an apparent contradiction in these laws: The fields belong to the farmers, but the entire harvest does not. To pious Israelites, the field is theirs and yet not theirs. It is private property, yet not an exclusive possession. That is because the Lord of the covenant community is the real owner of the land. Israelites recognize that their property is ultimately a gift of God that they hold on loan, as it were. In Leviticus 25:23 God says, "The land is mine, and you are strangers and resident aliens with me." Hence the basis for the gleaning law is not only humanitarian but also theological. It protects the poor, but it is also rooted in that story that shapes the identity of the covenant community: "I am the LORD your God, who brought you out of the land of Egypt" (Deut. 5:6; compare 24:22).

Notice what this social ethic rooted in a spiritual narrative does to the commandment on stealing. If stealing is taking what is not yours, and if even your private property is ultimately not yours, then even taking what *is* yours can be stealing, if you take it without regard for the health of the wider community. Today we are increasingly recognizing that the community in which we live is no longer simply a village or city or nation, but the entire earth, with all its people and ecosystems. What does the Eighth Commandment mean in the context of the "global village"? What especially does it mean for affluent North Americans? In such a village, individual acts that seem harmless have enormous social consequences when multiplied by the millions. If your part of the village uses 80 percent of the village's energy (as does the United States), the rest of the village may think that you are a den of thieves. In this sense, it is possible to steal simply by the way one lives. The lifestyle of a consumer culture may be gained by ecological theft.

In a newspaper survey on sin 49 percent of the people polled thought it was a sin to fudge on one's golf score. Only 2 percent thought that eating red meat was a sin. That is because most of us think of eating as a purely private matter. It involves our personal health but not our communal health. Yet because of the enormous quantities of resources that it takes to produce beef, one could argue that eating red meat is far more harmful to many more people than cheating on a golf game. From a social point of view, stealing becomes something that involves virtually all of us, demanding that we examine the way we live in order to minimize our impact on the earth, which is a gift of God that belongs to all.

LYING
Deuteronomy 5:20

5:20 **Neither shall you bear false witness against your neighbor.**

The original focus of the Ninth Commandment was on courtroom testimony. It prohibited a witness from giving false testimony in a judicial proceeding. In short, it forbade perjury. Ancient Israel was well aware of the dangers of false witnesses (see Deut. 17:6–7; 19:15–21). The story of Jezebel's treachery in obtaining the land of Naboth is a case in point (1 Kings 21).

I see no good reason to limit the significance of the Ninth Commandment; we may extend it to include virtually all lying, but especially that which is damaging to one's neighbor (whether the neighbor is an individual or an entire society). The commandment then becomes a prohibition against deception. It would affect questions like the following: Is it justifiable for a physician to withhold information from a patient? Is it ever right for a lawyer to allow a client to lie? At what point does advertising become false? Is it fair for a student to submit a short story when it has been edited by her novelist mother? What if your boss at work asks you to sign a report that contains false information? How free should political leaders be to appeal to "national security" when lying to the public? Lying frequently takes place in personal relationships—between friends, between parents and children, between spouses, within extended families, in larger communities (even churches). (See Bok, *Lying*, 1978.)

Most ethicists would recognize that at times a lie is not only excusable but desirable, especially when it is the only way to avoid harm. A classic case would be the situation in which a Nazi officer asked a resident if there were any Jews in the neighborhood, and the resident lied and said no. In such a situation, dishonesty is honorable; honesty is abominable. But we shall focus on those situations, both public and private, in which lies are seriously damaging to society and to personal relationships.

Skepticism about the honesty of public officials in our country is at an all-time high. One of the reasons for this skepticism is that the American public knows they have been lied to by government figures at the highest levels. In ancient Israel the hall of justice was the city gate (see Ruth 4:1–12; Deut. 21:19; 22:15). It is ironic that our culture has coined the suffix "-gate" to refer to the *in*justice of government officials' lying to the public, beginning, of course, with "Watergate." We also have coined the word "disinformation."

But if lying happens at the highest levels of public office, it also happens close to home. In family relationships lying often takes the form of mutual deception in which the people involved tacitly agree to "live" the lie. It may be to hide some unpleasant secret, such as child abuse or alcoholism. It may be to deny some painful memory. It may be to maintain an illusion. But whatever the reason—even well intentioned—such mutual deception almost always imprisons the family within a vicious cycle of falsehood. When Biff, a character in the play *Death of a Salesman*, says, "We never told the truth for ten minutes in this house," he speaks for many families.

Lying happens in many circumstances. Parents often do it when they deny a child's irresponsibility. Teachers do it when they pass a failing student. Colleagues do it when they habitually "cover" for a fellow's mistakes. Yet in the end such lies usually imprison those who tell them and those for whose benefit they are told. Such deceits often turn *against* the "neighbor" whom they intend to help, and so become like the damaging "lying witness" of the Ninth Commandment.

But when people have the courage to confront the truth, they claim the capability of becoming free. Indeed, dramas often turn on what we call a "moment of truth," a moment when the characters are forced, sometimes painfully, to look at the reality behind all their illusions, to see who they really are. That is also the stuff of transformations in counseling and therapy, and of "conversion" in spiritual development. Conversion may be understood as a "collision" with the truth about our lives. The very purpose of religious traditions is to confront us with this truth, by showing us models of what true humanity is like. "You will know the truth," says Jesus, "and the truth will make you free" (John 8:32).

COVETING
Deuteronomy 5:21

5:21 **Neither shall you covet your neighbor's wife.**
    Neither shall you desire your neighbor's house, or field, or male or female slave, or ox, or donkey, or anything that belongs to your neighbor.

The best time of the year to meditate on this commandment is during Advent. One of the best biblical stories to read as a companion is in Numbers 11. In that story, the Israelites are traveling through the wilderness and they grow tired of eating manna and demand meat. The people's craving for meat has a double irony: (1) It prevents their continuing gratitude for what they have—the manna that, when it first appeared, they greeted joyfully as a miraculous gift of God (Exodus 16); and (2) It blocks their memory of the reason why they are where they are—they have been liberated from Egyptian slavery and are on their way through the wilderness to "the land of milk and honey." Their craving for better *food* overwhelms their previous desire for *freedom*. Their desire for material things replaces one of humankind's deepest spiritual needs.

Coveting is a desire that is out of proportion to one's need. When ancient Israel put together a list of the ten most essential "do's and don'ts," coveting was one of the don'ts. Deuteronomy 5:21 uses two words, "covet" and "desire" or "crave." Going beyond our culture's common understanding, "covet" includes the connotation of an action that follows upon wanting something. The prohibition "do not covet" means do not desire something and then go out and get it. David desired the wife of Uriah, and he got her, along with a lot of trouble. The word "crave" is even more basic. It refers primarily to a mental attitude rather than an action.

Thus the commandment attempts to govern not only what we do but even what we think and feel. The law tries to prevent us from even thinking, "I wish I had that house, that car, that jacket, those shoes," when those things are disproportionate to our need. The law is trying to shape not only our actions but our very consciousness. Hence the law is not simply an ethical rule; it is also, and much more profoundly, a spiritual guide (again, the basic meaning of *torah*).

Coveting is a spiritual disease whose underlying cause is insecurity. Again, the story from Numbers illustrates the problem: If only we had meat to eat, then we would be happy. Craving means trading true happiness (freedom in the promised land) for momentary pleasure (meat to eat) even at the risk of losing oneself (the return to Egyptian slavery; note the name given to the setting of the story—"Graves of Craving," Num. 11:34).

Unfortunately, we live in a culture where craving is a virtue and is encouraged as the major stimulus for economic well-being. In a sense, a commercial economy depends on craving. It want us to "shop 'til we drop." While the Ten Commandments tell us not to crave our neighbors' possessions, television bombards us with thousands of images of people whose possessions we simply must have. As a popular proverb puts it, "Enough is what most of us would be glad to have if we didn't see others with more."

The caption at the top of a recent half-page newspaper ad by a bank asks, "So how do I pay for it?" Pictures and text give some examples: "I know exactly the car I want. I know the model. I know the options. Even the color and choice of fabric for the seats. What I don't know is: How do I pay for it?" Other examples are: the expenses for a big wedding, a remodeled kitchen, "the perfect house," a motorboat—each ending with the question, "How do I pay for it?" Then, in the bottom righthand corner appear the prominent words, "JUST ASK," and the bank's name.

If controlling adult craving is difficult, stifling the craving of children is all but impossible. Children are cravers by nature. Psychologists suggest that children's "needs" often mask their desire for love and acceptance, and those are deeply spiritual desires that cannot be met by the provision of one material thing after another.

"You shall not covet." To follow this commandment is to choose deprivation of material wants in order to gain the increase of spiritual gifts. This is what Jesus meant when he warned, "Take care! Be on your guard against all kinds of greed [RSV, 'covetousness']; for one's life does not consist in the abundance of possessions" (Luke 12:15). That is why he advised people to seek the realm of God before all *things* (Matt. 6:33), and why he said that "where your treasure is, there your heart will be also" (Matt. 6:21). Those whose basic needs are met will often have to shun unneeded things in order to receive spiritual gifts such as creativity, play, truth, peacefulness, wisdom, trust, and love. Young children who spend five minutes with a fancy new electronic toy, then occupy hours with the cardboard box that contained it, exhibit instinctive self-deprivation in favor of a spiritual gift—the exercise of their imagination. People who decide not to purchase a cordless phone to take with them to the garden, or the golf course, or fishing, exhibit self-deprivation in favor of the spiritual gift of peacefulness. The family that spends an hour playing cards or a board game together instead of watching television exhibits self-deprivation in favor of the spiritual gift of deepening relationships.

Perhaps, then, the positive side of the Tenth Commandment appears in the advice of Henry David Thoreau when he said, "Simplify! Simplify!" a preachment that he practiced by living a simple life in his cabin at Walden Pond. Indeed, simplicity is the spiritual discipline that one adopts when one chooses not to covet. Simplicity is the substance of the ancient proverb, "wisdom . . . is better than silver" (Prov. 3:13–14), and the modern proverb, "less is more." As an old Shaker hymn puts it, " 'tis a gift to be simple, 'tis a gift to be free." (See Foster, *Celebration*, 1978, chap. 6.)

6. The Peril of Affluence

Deuteronomy 8:1–20

8:1 **This entire commandment that I command you today you must diligently observe, so that you may live and increase, and go in and occupy the
land that the LORD promised on oath to your ancestors.**[2] **Remember the long
way that the LORD your God has led you these forty years in the wilderness,
in order to humble you, testing you to know what was in your heart, whether
or not you would keep his commandments.** [3] **He humbled you by letting you
hunger, then by feeding you with manna, with which neither you nor your
ancestors were acquainted, in order to make you understand that one does
not live by bread alone, but by every word that comes from the mouth of
the LORD.** [4] **The clothes on your back did not wear out and your feet did not
swell these forty years.** [5] **Know then in your heart that as a parent disciplines
a child so the LORD your God disciplines you.** [6] **Therefore keep the commandments of the LORD your God, by walking in his ways and by fearing
him.** [7] **For the LORD your God is bringing you into a good land, a land with
flowing streams, with springs and underground waters welling up in valleys
and hills,** [8] **a land of wheat and barley, of vines and fig trees and pome-
granates, a land of olive trees and honey,** [9] **a land where you may eat bread
without scarcity, where you will lack nothing, a land whose stones are iron
and from whose hills you may mine copper.** [10] **You shall eat your fill and
bless the LORD your God for the good land that he has given you.**

[11] **Take care that you do not forget the LORD your God, by failing to keep
his commandments, his ordinances, and his statutes, which I am commanding you today.** [12] **When you have eaten your fill and have built fine houses
and live in them,** [13] **and when your herds and flocks have multiplied, and
your silver and gold is multiplied, and all that you have is multiplied,** [14] **then
do not exalt yourself, forgetting the LORD your God, who brought you out
of the land of Egypt, out of the house of slavery,** [15] **who led you through the
great and terrible wilderness, an arid wasteland with poisonous snakes and
scorpions. He made water flow for you from flint rock,** [16] **and fed you in the
wilderness with manna that your ancestors did not know, to humble you and
to test you, and in the end to do you good.** [17] **Do not say to yourself, "My
power and the might of my own hand have gotten me this wealth."** [18] **But**

remember the LORD your God, for it is he who gives you power to get
wealth, so that he may confirm his covenant that he swore to your ancestors, as he is doing today. [19] If you do forget the LORD your God and follow
other gods to serve and worship them, I solemnly warn you today that you
shall surely perish. [20] Like the nations that the LORD is destroying before you,
so shall you perish, because you would not obey the voice of the LORD your
God.

(The best liturgical season to read this text would be Lent, when the
story of Jesus' temptation in the wilderness and his quotation of Deuteronomy 8:5 appear in many lectionaries. But it is applicable to any time
in which people find themselves living the good life, a situation that the
author finds highly desirable but also highly dangerous.)

LIFE: MATERIAL GOODS AND
SPIRITUAL BELONGINGS

Probably because Jesus quotes it, the line in 8:5 is one of the best-known
Bible sayings: "one does not live by bread alone, but by every word that
comes from the mouth of the Lord." Here the word "bread" stands for
food in general. The saying is in no way a denial of the goodness of material things. It certainly does *not* mean that we have no need for food. The
author shows a tremendous appreciation for the blessings of life. Bread
and wine, herds and flocks, silver and gold, are not intrinsically evil, and
enjoyment of them should not be soured by a false piety that separates the
spiritual and the material. The text says that we do not live by bread alone;
but it does not say that we live by the word of God alone. The life that
God gives to us includes both word and bread.

But the saying does suggest that life in its fullest sense requires something more than physical nourishment. In order to be fully alive, we need
something more than food, and, by extension, something more than any
thing, any material good. What we need is to remember the connection
between our spirits and *the* Spirit. That connection is what gives us life in
the fullest sense, just as it gave life to the first human being—from the
mouth of God (Gen. 2:7).

While Moses is speaking to the children of the wilderness generation,
the author is speaking to people who have been in the land for centuries.
He is speaking to people who are living the good life. This interpretive
perspective is important to prevent the conclusion that Deuteronomy (especially vv. 1–6) provides a theological justification for poverty or hunger.

Elsewhere Deuteronomy insists that hunger would not exist in a just so-ciety (as in 15:4; 24:19–22). Here the author looks back to the deprivations of the wilderness in order to emphasize the meaning of the story for the present, and in doing so he engages in exaggeration (for instance, 8:4).

The text consists of four units. Verses 1–6 focus on the wilderness ex-perience, verses 7–10 on the promised land, verses 11–18 on both wilder-ness and promised land, and verses 19–20 provide a conclusion. First, Is-rael is told to remember the time of the wilderness when scarcity made them totally dependent on God. Then they are projected into the good land (vv. 7–10) where scarcity will be replaced by abundance and they will eat their fill. Then in verses 11–20 Moses combines references to both the good land and the wilderness, warning of what will happen if Israel for-gets the past.

DEPRAVED BY ABUNDANCE

The irony is that both the wilderness experience and life in the promised land, both hunger and fullness, are tests, and the greater test is that of full-ness. In the wilderness, the people were tested by hunger, and they often failed the test. They refused to rely on the "daily bread" of fresh manna, and instead tried to hoard more than they needed (see Exod. 16). Yet, even as they failed the test, the manna did not fail *them*, so they learned about the grace of God. In their radical dependence, they learned that life itself comes from God.

But in the promised land they will have more than enough food. They will be full. They will be content. Then comes the greater test, for mate-rial contentment leads easily to spiritual atrophy. The author expresses this spiritual degeneration in terms of remembering and forgetting: Re-membering what they might prefer to forget is life (Deut. 8:1, 3); forget-ting the past cuts off the future and leads to death (v. 19). Once they have "arrived" they will forget where they came from. They will not need God any more. It is sort of the opposite of the proverb that there are no athe-ists in foxholes: There are no believers in Fat City. When material life is abundant, it is easy to forget the source of *all* life. In that forgetting, Israel will fall prey to the peril of affluence. As Augustine said of the collapse of Rome, they will be depraved by abundance and not chastened by adver-sity.

The central concern of the text is the inner attitude, or "heart," of the people, as in verses 2, 5, 14 ("exalt" is "lift up your heart"), 17 (literally, "say in your heart"). Again we hear echoes of the Shema (6:5–6). The greatest danger in forgetting the wilderness lesson of dependence on God's grace is the growth of a false sense of self-sufficiency and independence.

The deepest irony appears in 8:17: "Do not say in your heart, 'My power and the might of my own hand have gotten me this wealth' " (my translation). A people who survived in the wilderness only because of God's grace, and who are living in the good land only because of God's gift (v. 10), now attributes their great fortune to their own hard work. "We have earned all this. We pulled ourselves up by our own bootstraps and we aren't obligated to anybody." The result is not only theological amnesia but also moral insensitivity—an inability to sympathize with those who have not made it (see especially chap. 24). Recent interviews with white, middle-class Americans indicate a similar attitude:

> [They] emphasized that they attained their present status in life through their own hard work, seldom mentioning the part played by their family, schooling, or the advantages that came to them from being middle class to start with. It is not that they would deny the contributions others have made to their success in life; what they deny is the moral relevance of those contributions. It is only insofar as they can claim that they have succeeded *through their own efforts* that they can feel they have deserved that achievement. (Bellah and others, *Habits of the Heart*, 1985, 198; see also especially pp. 294–96 on "The Poverty of Affluence.")

Deuteronomy 8 concludes with another warning about worshiping other gods, again, a reference to the First and Second Commandments. The connection at first seems awkward, but Israel often attributed the abundance of the land to the Baals instead of to the Lord (see Hosea 2). When we think of "other gods" as alternative centers of value in our own lives, we can see how the connection also makes sense for us. Failure to recognize the source "from whom all blessings flow" is spiritually lethal (Deut. 8:20). Instead, genuine enjoyment of the good things of life includes gratitude to God and, as subsequent laws will show, generosity to neighbors.

7. The Broken Covenant
Deuteronomy 9:1–10:11

9:1 Hear, O Israel! You are about to cross the Jordan today, to go in and dispossess nations larger and mightier than you, great cities, fortified to the heavens, ² a strong and tall people, the offspring of the Anakim, whom you know. You have heard it said of them, "Who can stand up to the Anakim?" ³ Know then today that the LORD your God is the one who crosses over before you as a devouring fire; he will defeat them and subdue them before you, so that you may dispossess and destroy them quickly, as the LORD has promised you.

⁴ When the LORD your God thrusts them out before you, do not say to yourself, "It is because of my righteousness that the LORD has brought me in to occupy this land"; it is rather because of the wickedness of these nations that the LORD is dispossessing them before you. ⁵ It is not because of your righteousness or the uprightness of your heart that you are going in to occupy their land; but because of the wickedness of these nations the LORD your God is dispossessing them before you, in order to fulfill the promise that the LORD made on oath to your ancestors, to Abraham, to Isaac, and to Jacob.

⁶ Know, then, that the LORD your God is not giving you this good land to occupy because of your righteousness; for you are a stubborn people. ⁷ Remember and do not forget how you provoked the LORD your God to wrath in the wilderness; you have been rebellious against the LORD from the day you came out of the land of Egypt until you came to this place.

⁸ Even at Horeb you provoked the LORD to wrath, and the LORD was so angry with you that he was ready to destroy you. ⁹ When I went up the mountain to receive the stone tablets, the tablets of the covenant that the LORD made with you, I remained on the mountain forty days and forty nights; I neither ate bread nor drank water. ¹⁰ And the LORD gave me the two stone tablets written with the finger of God; on them were all the words that the LORD had spoken to you at the mountain out of the fire on the day of the assembly. ¹¹ At the end of forty days and forty nights the LORD gave me the two stone tablets, the tablets of the covenant. ¹² Then the LORD said to me, "Get up, go down quickly from here, for your people whom you have

brought from Egypt have acted corruptly. They have been quick to turn from the way that I commanded them; they have cast an image for themselves." 13 Furthermore the LORD said to me, "I have seen that this people is indeed a stubborn people. 14 Let me alone that I may destroy them and blot out their name from under heaven; and I will make of you a nation mightier and more numerous than they."

15 So I turned and went down from the mountain, while the mountain was ablaze; the two tablets of the covenant were in my two hands. 16 Then I saw that you had indeed sinned against the LORD your God, by casting for yourselves an image of a calf; you had been quick to turn from the way that the LORD had commanded you. 17 So I took hold of the two tablets and flung them from my two hands, smashing them before your eyes. 18 Then I lay prostrate before the LORD as before, forty days and forty nights; I neither ate bread nor drank water, because of all the sin you had committed, provoking the LORD by doing what was evil in his sight. 19 For I was afraid that the anger that the LORD bore against you was so fierce that he would destroy you. But the LORD listened to me that time also. 20 The LORD was so angry with Aaron that he was ready to destroy him, but I interceded also on behalf of Aaron at that same time. 21 Then I took the sinful thing you had made, the calf, and burned it with fire and crushed it, grinding it thoroughly, until it was reduced to dust; and I threw the dust of it into the stream that runs down the mountain.

22 At Taberah also, and at Massah, and at Kibroth-hattaavah, you provoked the LORD to wrath. 23 And when the LORD sent you from Kadesh-barnea, saying, "Go up and occupy the land that I have given you," you rebelled against the command of the LORD your God, neither trusting him nor obeying him. 24 You have been rebellious against the LORD as long as he has known you.

25 Throughout the forty days and forty nights that I lay prostrate before the LORD when the LORD intended to destroy you, 26 I prayed to the LORD and said, "LORD GOD, do not destroy the people who are your very own possession, whom you redeemed in your greatness, whom you brought out of Egypt with a mighty hand. 27 Remember your servants, Abraham, Isaac, and Jacob; pay no attention to the stubbornness of this people, their wickedness and their sin, 28 otherwise the land from which you have brought us might say, 'Because the LORD was not able to bring them into the land that he promised them, and because he hated them, he has brought them out to let them die in the wilderness.' 29 For they are the people of your very own possession, whom you brought out by your great power and by your outstretched arm."

10:1 At that time the LORD said to me, "Carve out two tablets of stone like the former ones, and come up to me on the mountain, and make an ark of wood. 2 I will write on the tablets the words that were on the former tablets, which you smashed, and you shall put them in the ark." 3 So I made an ark of acacia wood, cut two tablets of stone like the former ones, and went up the mountain with the two tablets in my hand. [4] Then he wrote on the tablets the same words as before, the ten commandments that the LORD had spoken to you on the mountain out of the fire on the day of the assembly; and the LORD gave them to me. [5] So I turned and came down from the mountain, and put the tablets in the ark that I had made; and there they are, as the LORD commanded me.

[6] (The Israelites journeyed from Beeroth Bene-jaakan to Moserah. There Aaron died, and there he was buried; his son Eleazar succeeded him as priest. [7] From there they journeyed to Gudgodah, and from Gudgodah to Jotbathah, a land with flowing streams. [8] At that time the LORD set apart the tribe of Levi to carry the ark of the covenant of the LORD, to stand before the LORD to minister to him, and to bless in his name, to this day. [9] Therefore Levi has no allotment or inheritance with his kindred; the LORD is his inheritance, as the LORD your God promised him.)

[10] I stayed on the mountain forty days and forty nights, as I had done the first time. And once again the LORD listened to me. The LORD was unwilling to destroy you. [11] The LORD said to me, "Get up, go on your journey at the head of the people, that they may go in and occupy the land that I swore to their ancestors to give them."

This section is marked off by the recurrence of the key phrase "Hear, O Israel!" (see also 6:4 and 5:1). The section is a companion to chapters 4 and 5 in that they too recapitulate events at Horeb. Here, though, the event is not the making, but the breaking, of the covenant between the Lord and Israel. Similarly, this section reminds us of the disastrous spy story in chapter 1 in that here too Israel came to the brink of destruction (see Numbers 13—14 as well as Exodus 32—34). Thus Deuteronomy 1—11, the introduction to the "statutes and ordinances" in chapters 12—26, is framed on either end by stories of urgent warning.

THE COVENANT BROKEN AND RESTORED

Deuteronomy 9:1–10:11 contains the following units: 9:1–3, 4–5, 6–24 (with subsections 6–7, 8–14, and 15–24); 9:25–10:9; and 10:10–11. The opening passage, 9:1–3, reminds us of chapter 7, with the promise of God's presence as warrior when Israel enters the land. The next passage, verses 4–5, turns to Israel's attitude regarding the conquest, a subject of both chapters 7 and 8. This focus is evident in 9:4 where "say to yourself" means "say in your heart," as in 7:17 and 8:17. In chapters 7 and 8 the problems were, respectively, unnecessary self-doubt before the conquest and unjustified self-sufficiency afterward. Here the potential problem is self-righteousness. When Israel has conquered the land, the people will be tempted to think that it was because of their goodness. In chapter 8 they attributed success to their own work; here they will attribute it to their worth.

The rejection of this possibility returns to the subject of Israel's election, already broached in 7:7–8. God is "dispossessing" the Canaanites for two reasons, one negative, one positive: negatively, because of the wickedness of the native inhabitants; positively, because of God's oath to the ancestors (see Gen. 12:1–3, etc.). Neither of these reasons has anything to do with Israel's merit. On the contrary, they are a "stubborn people" (Deut. 9:6, 13; literally, "stiff-necked"). Using contrasting key words, Moses now calls on them to "remember and not forget" their past, how they have been "rebellious" from the moment they left Egypt to the moment he is speaking (9:7).

The programmatic accusation in 9:7 implies that Israel possesses the land of Canaan only because of God's grace. Their history is evidence that they can never claim to be the chosen people because of their superior morality, piety, faith, or obedience—indeed, because of any quality of their character. Just as 7:7–8 says that God did not choose them because of their size, so here Moses says that God did not choose them because of their merit. That, after all, is what grace means: unearned love. But Moses does not so much argue this point as narrate it: he retells the story of the broken covenant (9:8–24).

The story of the molten calf in 9:12–16 has its counterpart in Exodus 32 and also in the spy story in Numbers 13—14 (for example, compare Deut. 9:14 with Exod. 32:10 and Num. 14:12). The calf story almost certainly reflects the religious innovation of King Jeroboam, the first ruler of northern Israel. In the ninth century, Jeroboam incorporated the popular bull symbol within the worship of the Lord in an attempt to provide an alternative to the symbols of ark and temple in Jerusalem, the capital of the southern kingdom from which Jeroboam and the northern tribes had separated (1 Kings 12:25–33; compare especially 1 Kings 12:28b with Exod. 32:4b). This act of royal presumption was judged by the Deuteronomic historians to be a fatal mistake, leading to the fall of the dynasty and ultimately to the destruction of Israel (see 1 Kings 13:34; 2 Kings 17, especially v. 16).

The account of the calf incident in Deuteronomy 9:12–16 differs from its counterparts in Exodus and Numbers in two ways. First, while both Exodus 32 and Numbers 13—14 contain divine threats of a complete destruction or abandonment of the people (Exod. 32:10; Num. 14:12),

Deuteronomy presents this threat only in the calf story, not in the spy story of chapter 1. That limitation may reiterate the legacy of Jeroboam, and also suggest that breach of covenant is more serious than lack of trust (compare Num. 14:11). Second, the account in Deuteronomy 9—10 is not so much the story of the golden calf as the story of a broken and restored covenant. Both are present, of course, in Exodus, but the emphasis here in the retelling falls on juridical process, and this process provides the narrative plot.

Deuteronomy 9—10 documents the legal procedure through which the treaty between the Lord and Israel is broken and then reinstated. The emphasis begins in 9:9–11, where repetition of "the stone tablets" and "the tablets of the covenant" serve to focus our attention on the treaty document. After the report of the calf and threat of destruction (vv. 12–14), the key phrases continue. Moses returns to the people with "the two tablets of the covenant" in hand (v. 15), then he flings "the two tablets," "smashing them before your eyes" (v. 17). The latter phrase emphasizes the people's witnessing of the formal renunciation of the treaty by Moses as God's representative.

Similarly, the repetition of "the (two) tablets" becomes almost wooden in 10:1–5 (seven times), and the key sentence reporting the rewriting of the treaty (10:4) is a mirror image of the initial making of the treaty in 9:10. Also Deuteronomy portrays the construction of the ark in the context of this incident in order to emphasize its role as the place for keeping the treaty document (in Exodus the ark is not made until well after this incident; contrast also the Levites in Deut. 10:8–9 and in Exod. 32:25–29).

Thus throughout the account our eyes are focused on the two tablets—the treaty document—and not on the golden calf. It is remarkable that Deuteronomy does not mention the phrase "these are your gods, O Israel, who brought you up out of the land of Egypt" (Exod. 32:4; 1 Kings 12:28). So great is the focus on the breaking and restoring of the covenant document that Deuteronomy gives up the chance to lecture against the worship of "other gods."

Another interesting feature of the Deuteronomic account is the way in which the details of Moses' intercession are given after the fact, and immediately before the reinstituting of the treaty. Deuteronomy 9:19b hints at God's relenting from the threat of destruction, but the content of Moses' intercessory prayer does not come until 9:25–29. Moses' speech is framed by references to Israel as God's "very own possession" (vv. 26 and 29), and includes appeals to God's promise to the ancestors (v. 27; note "remember"), and even to God's reputation (v. 28; compare Exod. 14:

11–12; Num. 14:3; Deut. 1:27). Then, immediately after Moses' appeal, God says to him, "Carve out two tablets of stone like the former ones" (Deut. 10:1). No punishment is meted out (compare Exod. 32:28) or projected as in Exodus 32:32, 34. There is no *immediate* reference to God's change of mind (compare Exod. 32:14). Moreover, the people play no role whatsoever in the covenant restitution, which occurs only in a private conversation between God and Moses on top of the mountain. The *people* have not confessed their sin or repented of it, nor is there any ritual of atonement (as perhaps in Exod. 32:20b). These attempts at reconciliation happen only through Moses.

Moses pleads, "pay no attention to . . . their sin" (Deut. 9:27), and God responds, "carve out two tablets of stone like the former ones." The abrupt shift suggests that reinstatement of the covenant itself is the beginning of divine forgiveness. Forgiveness is not something outside or beyond the covenant; it is expressed by the *renewal* of the covenant. Now when Moses issues "the statutes and ordinances" (Deut. 12:1), it will mean the stipulations of the covenant given to Israel *despite* its sin, despite its refusal to hear, remember, and obey. Israel is the "stiff-necked" vassal to whom the Great King has extended continued benevolence despite rebellion. Nowhere is it more clear than here that God has given the covenant (including the specific laws) for Israel's benefit, that *the law itself* is thus an expression of divine grace, which God is therefore not willing to withdraw.

Moses approaches the end of his prologue, his passionate sermon calling for obedience, only to face the fact of disobedience. But more inconceivable even than this disobedience is the other fact that the covenant is restored. Once again we see the tension between what the covenant required and what God would allow. God is unwilling to destroy (Deut. 10:10; see Hos. 11:8–9).

Yet again the story of the broken covenant provides little room for contentment, much less for immunity. When Moses is recommissioned to lead the people up *to* the land (Deut. 10:11), we are reminded that after they enter the land, Moses will no longer be with them. Moses is now not only the mediator of the covenant but also the intercessor for atonement, and we are left to wonder what will happen in the face of disobedience when the intercessor is no more.

Thus the story of the broken covenant ends much like the spy story of chapter 1. Despite the emphasis on the grace of God, both sections are intended as a note of warning. Deuteronomy holds together the threat of divine wrath and that strange, inconceivable fact of divine grace, "amazing grace."

8. "If You Will Only Heed"
Deuteronomy 10:12–11:32

10:12 So now, O Israel, what does the LORD your God require of you? Only to fear the LORD your God, to walk in all his ways, to love him, to serve the LORD your God with all your heart and with all your soul, 13 and to keep the commandments of the LORD your God and his decrees that I am commanding you today, for your own well-being. 14 Although heaven and the heaven of heavens belong to the LORD your God, the earth with all that is in it, 15 yet the LORD set his heart in love on your ancestors alone and chose you, their descendants after them, out of all the peoples, as it is today. 16 Circumcise, then, the foreskin of your heart, and do not be stubborn any longer. 17 For the LORD your God is God of gods and LORD of lords, the great God, mighty and awesome, who is not partial and makes no bribe, 18 who executes justice for the orphan and the widow, and who loves the strangers, providing them food and clothing. 19 You shall also love the stranger, for you were strangers in the land of Egypt. 20 You shall fear the LORD your God; him alone you shall worship; to him you shall hold fast, and by his name you shall swear. 21 He is your praise; he is your God, who has done for you these great and awesome things that your own eyes have seen. 22 Your ancestors went down to Egypt seventy persons; and now the LORD your God has made you as numerous as the stars in heaven.

11:1 You shall love the LORD your God, therefore, and keep his charge, his decrees, his ordinances, and his commandments always. 2 Remember today that it was not your children (who have not known or seen the discipline of the LORD your God), but it is you who must acknowledge his greatness, his mighty hand and his outstretched arm, 3 his signs and his deeds that he did in Egypt to Pharaoh, the king of Egypt, and to all his land; 4 what he did to the Egyptian army, to their horses and chariots, how he made the water of the Red Sea flow over them as they pursued you, so that the LORD has destroyed them to this day; 5 what he did to you in the wilderness, until you came to this place; 6 and what he did to Dathan and Abiram, sons of Eliab son of Reuben, how in the midst of all Israel the earth opened its mouth and swallowed them up, along with their households, their tents, and every living being in their company; ⁷ for it is your own eyes that have seen every great deed that the LORD did.

⁸ Keep, then, this entire commandment that I am commanding you today, so that you may have strength to go in and occupy the land that you are crossing over to occupy, ⁹ and so that you may live long in the land that the LORD swore to your ancestors to give them and to their descendants, a land flowing with milk and honey. ¹⁰ For the land that you are about to enter to occupy is not like the land of Egypt, from which you have come, where you sow your seed and irrigate by foot like a vegetable garden. ¹¹ But the land that you are crossing over to occupy is a land of hills and valleys, watered by rain from the sky, ¹² a land that the LORD your God looks after. The eyes of the LORD your God are always on it, from the beginning of the year to the end of the year.

¹³ If you will only heed his every commandment that I am commanding you today—loving the LORD your God, and serving him with all your heart and with all your soul—¹⁴ then he will give the rain for your land in its season, the early rain and the later rain, and you will gather in your grain, your wine, and your oil; ¹⁵ and he will give grass in your fields for your livestock, and you will eat your fill. ¹⁶ Take care, or you will be seduced into turning away, serving other gods and worshiping them, ¹⁷ for then the anger of the LORD will be kindled against you and he will shut up the heavens, so that there will be no rain and the land will yield no fruit; then you will perish quickly off the good land that the LORD is giving you.

¹⁸ You shall put these words of mine in your heart and soul, and you shall bind them as a sign on your hand, and fix them as an emblem on your forehead. ¹⁹Teach them to your children, talking about them when you are at home and when you are away, when you lie down and when you rise. ²⁰ Write them on the doorposts of your house and on your gates, ²¹ so that your days and the days of your children may be multiplied in the land that the LORD swore to your ancestors to give them, as long as the heavens are above the earth.

²² If you will diligently observe this entire commandment that I am commanding you, loving the LORD your God, walking in all his ways, and holding fast to him, ²³ then the LORD will drive out all these nations before you, and you will dispossess nations larger and mightier than yourselves. ²⁴ Every place on which you set foot shall be yours; your territory shall extend from the wilderness to the Lebanon and from the River, the river Euphrates, to the Western Sea. ²⁵ No one will be able to stand against you; the LORD your God will put the fear and dread of you on all the land on which you set foot, as he promised you.

²⁶ See, I am setting before you today a blessing and a curse: ²⁷ the blessing, if you obey the commandments of the LORD your God that I am commanding you today; ²⁸ and the curse, if you do not obey the commandments

of the LORD your God, but turn from the way that I am commanding you today, to follow other gods that you have not known.

²⁹ When the LORD your God has brought you into the land that you are
entering to occupy, you shall set the blessing on Mount Gerizim and the
curse on Mount Ebal. ³⁰ As you know, they are beyond the Jordan, some dis-
tance to the west, in the land of the Canaanites who live in the Arabah, opposite Gilgal, beside the oak of Moreh. ³¹ When you cross the Jordan to go
in to occupy the land that the LORD your God is giving you, and when you
occupy it and live in it, ³² you must diligently observe all the statutes and
ordinances that I am setting before you today.

Here Moses concludes the prologue to the "statutes and ordinances" in
Deuteronomy 12—26. This section is not tightly structured but flows together in homiletic cadences. Nevertheless, we can discern major shifts as
follows: 10:12–11:7 focus on the past, particularly the Lord's dealings with
the ancestors of Genesis, in the exodus, and in the wilderness experiences.
Then 11:8–25 turn to the future, focusing on the land of Canaan. The unit
concludes with the promise of blessings and the threat of curses
(11:26–32). Like much of Deuteronomy, then, this concluding exhortation is concerned to apply the lessons of the past to the requirements of
the future, so that the future will *be* one of blessing and not curse.

LOOKING BACK, LOOKING AHEAD

Deuteronomy 10:12–11:32 is retrospective not only of events in Israel's
past but also of the preceding chapters in Deuteronomy itself. We hear
repeated echoes of the First Commandment of 5:7 and the Shema of 6:4–5
(as in 10:12; 11:13, 16, 18), and indeed of all of 6:2–9 in 11:18–19. We hear
again references to Israel's election in terms of 7:7 (10:15). We see the
"stiff-necked" motif of chapters 9—10 in 10:16. The almost lyrical descriptions of the land, especially 11:11–12, recall chapter 8, and expectations of the conquest resemble especially chapter 7 (compare 11:23 and
7:1). If the "so now" of 4:1 seemed appropriate, the "so now" of 10:12 is
even more so. Except for brief references to the exodus (as in 16:12),
Moses will not again retell stories from Israel's past. Story time is over;
now it is time for the rules (chaps. 12—26).

But, as much of the preceding chapters have said, unless these stories
are remembered and personally absorbed, the rules will be groundless and
inexplicable. In a sense, then, chapters 1—11 are to the rest of Deuteron-

omy what the prologue to the Ten Commandments (5:6) is to the commandments themselves. Life itself depends on the memory of those stories that all have their center in the grand central story, and issue in the great commandment.

Similarly, the unit of 10:12–11:32 is prospective not only of the entrance into Canaan but also of chapters 12—28. Again, there is a literary as well as a historical connection. The prospective nature is best seen in 10:12–22. This passage has the following structure:

exclusive obedience to the Lord (vv. 12–13)
    God cosmic and personal with Israel (vv. 14–15)
        negative command (v. 16)
    God cosmic and personal with others (vv. 17–18)
        positive command (v. 19)
exclusive obedience to the Lord (vv. 20–22)

The "so now" in 10:12 leads directly into a repetition of the Shema ("love the Lord") and a call for obedience to the commandments. Next, Israel is commanded not to repeat their "stubborn" ways (literally, "do not stiffen your neck again," v. 16), recalling the broken covenant story. Then God is again described, in verse 17, as *the* cosmic power, the "God of gods and Lord of lords," yet as a personal God who also attends to the needs of the most vulnerable human beings (orphans, widows, and "strangers," that is, resident aliens). Now Israel is commanded: "You shall also love the stranger, for you were strangers in the land of Egypt" (v. 19). The passage concludes with further exhortation on the exclusive worship of the Lord (vv. 20–22).

LOVING GOD, LOVING NEIGHBOR

There is a remarkable connection in Deuteronomy 10:12–11:32 between cosmic power and personal presence, but also between Israel and those whom the French would call *les misérables* (the pitiable ones). The *Book of Worship* of the United Church of Christ has a prayer that describes God as "close to us as breathing and distant as the farthest star." This is the way this passage in Deuteronomy describes God, with beautiful irony. God is described as a cosmic power of utter transcendence, yet at the same time as a personal God who has "fallen in love" with Israel, an expression that approximates what the Hebrew of "set his heart in love" means in 10:15 and 7:7. The romantic connotation (see Gen. 34:8; Deut. 21:11) here is something like the prince who has everything choosing the lowly scullery maid Cinderella. With such wonder and awe does Moses describe God's wanting to be the God of Israel.

But even more remarkable is that this same cosmic power, the "God of gods," cares intimately for the needs of the powerless, not just of Israel but of all, even those who are not Israelites. God "executes justice" for those who were easily mistreated in the ancient Near East. And *Israel* is commanded also to "love" these, just as God loves them. In short, 10:12–22 ties together the love of God that dominates the preceding chapters with the love of neighbor that is central to what follows, especially chapter 15; 16:9–12, 18–20; chapters 22—24). Chapters 1—9 have been concerned primarily with the vertical relationship between the Lord and Israel, with theology strictly construed. What follows certainly continues that concern but also takes up the horizontal relationships within the covenant community and even between covenant members and nonmembers, that is, it takes up ethics. If chapters 1—11 focus on love as obedience to God, chapters 12—26 include love as justice within the human community (compare Paul's move from Romans 1—11 to Romans 12—16). If the rules that follow require the stories that precede, so the stories require the rules for completion.

Finally, Deuteronomy 10:12–11:32 is both retrospective and prospective in that it reiterates various motivations for obedience already cited and concludes with an explicit reference to blessing and curse, looking forward to the extended sanctions in chapters 27—28. I will discuss the theology of blessing and curse more extensively when we come to those chapters, but for now we can simply recognize the many different motivations, sometimes not completely compatible, that Deuteronomy offers for obedience.

Positively, there are promises of general "well-being" (10:13), "strength" (11:8), long life (11:9, 21), military victory (11:22–25), and rain (11:13–14). Negatively, there are threats of destruction (10:6) and of drought (11:6–17). Note that the positive outweighs the negative. But most profoundly, the primary motivation is a sense of gratitude that comes from being loved unconditionally and even despite one's shortcomings, a gratitude rooted in the stories of God's care and faithfulness in the past, seen especially in the immediate connection with chapters 9—10, as well as in 10:14–15, 21–22; 11:2–5. It is primarily out of thankfulness for grace unearned, for redemption without precondition, for forgiveness undeserved, and for a land given without merit that Israel is called to "diligently observe all the statutes and ordinances that I am setting before you today" (11:32).

9. Camp Meeting

Deuteronomy 12:1–7

12:1 **These are the statutes and ordinances that you must diligently observe in the land that the LORD, the God of your ancestors, has given you to occupy all the days that you live on the earth.**

² **You must demolish completely all the places where the nations whom you are about to dispossess served their gods, on the mountain heights, on the hills, and under every leafy tree. ³ Break down their altars, smash their pillars, burn their sacred poles with fire, and hew down the idols of their gods, and thus blot out their name from their places. ⁴ You shall not worship the LORD your God in such ways. ⁵ But you shall seek the place that the LORD your God will choose out of all your tribes as his habitation to put his name there. You shall go there, ⁶ bringing there your burnt offerings and your sacrifices, your tithes and your donations, your votive gifts, your freewill offerings, and the firstlings of your herds and flocks. ⁷ And you shall eat there in the presence of the LORD your God, you and your households together, rejoicing in all the undertakings in which the LORD your God has blessed you.**

Deuteronomy 12 begins the "statutes and ordinances" that continue until the end of chapter 26. The framework to chapter 12 (vv. 2–4 and 29–32) shows that it is a practical extension of the warnings about engaging in alien religious practices that are forbidden in chapter 7. As 7:6 emphasized, Israel's status as the Lord's holy people requires the rejection of the religious practices and customs of the Canaanites. The ultimate concern again is the danger of being seduced into the worship of other gods and disobeying the First and Second Commandments. This concern is not merely theoretical but projects into the past (Moses' time) as warning what happened in the future (time of the kings)—a correlation evident from numerous editorial condemnations within the Deuteronomistic History (compare, for example, 12:2 with 1 Kings 3:23; 2 Kings 16:4; 7:10).

One way to prevent the imitation of foreign cultic practices is to limit and control where and how Israel's worship may take place. This is the purpose of Deuteronomy 12. The negative command prohibits using Canaanite worship places and forms; the positive command limits Israelite worship places. Israelites are not permitted to worship anywhere they please (for example, in each local community), but are required to "seek the place that the Lord your God will choose out of all your tribes as his habitation to put his name there" (v. 5).

It is not clear whether this means that there is only one place for authorized worship for all of the tribes, or only one place at a time, or even one place for each region. In early times, places like Shiloh may have been such a central sanctuary (as in Josh. 18:1); after Solomon built the Jerusalem temple, it would certainly have been "the place" intended by Deuteronomy in this law. At any rate, all religious ceremonies are restricted to the central sanctuary, where, presumably, the priests would keep a watchful eye and maintain orthodoxy in worship. The bulk of chapter 12 (vv. 15–28) distinguishes between types of secular food preparation and eating that may be practiced anywhere, as opposed to sacred preparation and eating that must be limited to the central sanctuary.

IMMANENCE AND TRANSCENDENCE

Deuteronomy developed a distinctly subtle theological understanding of the nature of God's presence at the sanctuary. At issue is the balance and tension between transcendence and immanence, between the Lord who is the cosmic "God of gods" (see 10:17) and yet the one who is in some sense present where the people gather to worship. Deuteronomy maintains the tension through its theology of the name of God. While the sanctuary is God's "habitation," it is really only so for God's name. God's own self is not there, only God's name. The Deuteronomic theology of the name may be intended to counteract what was perceived as the Canaanite understanding of a sanctuary, namely, that the god in a real sense "lived" at the geographical place, particularly on mountaintops and at "leafy trees" (v. 2; the latter a rare phenomenon in ancient Palestine). Such places, in fact, are elsewhere associated with Israelite traditions (as in Gen. 12:6; Exod. 3:1).

Moreover, alternative ways of understanding the Lord's presence at the sanctuary included much more concrete and dramatic media. Cloud and fire, perhaps related to burning incense, manifested God's sanctifying presence at the dedication of the tabernacle and of Solomon's temple

(Exod. 40:34–35; 1 Kings 8:10–11, respectively), and the same imagery is often associated with the sacred ark (Num. 10:33–34; 1 Kings 8:6–8). Of course, even these visible media obscured God's presence as much as they manifested it.

Deuteronomy preferred to think of God's name as the manifestation of God's presence. References to the central sanctuary as the place of God's name occur repeatedly (Deut. 14:23; 16:2, 5–7, 11, 15, 16; 17:8). We can see the concept of a name as a substitute for personal presence on the human level in a report about Absalom. Anticipating (correctly) that he would die without children to continue his name, Absalom erected a pillar and "called [it] after his own name" (2 Sam. 18:18). Similarly, Deuteronomy thinks of the central sanctuary as the place where the Lord's name stands for the Lord's presence, since the Lord cannot—or rather, will not—be there in any complete or ultimate sense.

Exactly how the name was understood to be present remains unclear. Certainly it did *not* involve a "pillar," an object closely associated with Canaanite worship (see Deut. 12:3). Most likely, the name was not evident in any concrete way. Yet it would be incorrect to think that the presence of the name was of merely token significance. For Deuteronomy the name of God represented God's power and authority as covenant lord. Destroying the Canaanite religious objects erased the names of *their* gods and thus, in effect, eliminated the gods themselves (v. 3).

That this name theology was intended to protect the Lord's transcendence is even more evident with a look at Solomon's temple dedication prayer in 1 Kings 8. While one tradition says that the temple is "a place for you to dwell in forever" (1 Kings 8:13), in the subsequent prayer Solomon qualifies this understanding by recognizing that God will not "dwell on the earth" (v. 27). God's name will be there, but heaven is God's real "dwelling place" (vv. 28–30).

THE GOD WHO "TENTS"

The word for "dwelling" in the preceding passages from 1 Kings usually refers to a fixed abode. In Deuteronomy 12:5 the word for "habitation" is a different word, one that refers primarily to impermanent abodes and specifically to tents. It is the root for the word "tabernacle," and refers to a type of dwelling that is movable. In a sense, therefore, Deuteronomy seems to have taken the notion of God's presence "moving about in a tent and a tabernacle" and translated it by the "tenting" of God's name at the central sanctuary (see 2 Sam. 7:5–7 and 13, which deals with the same theological problem). The result is a notion of divine presence that is real but also tentative: it is beyond human control, utterly dependent on God's selection ("the place that the Lord your God will choose" [12:5]), and God's presence can be withdrawn just as one pulls up tent stakes and moves away.

The implicit conditionality of God's presence at the central sanctuary thus provides an appropriate cultic counterpart to the covenant sanctions. God is "there" only when the worshipers are righteous and just. When they are not, then God cannot be found no matter how ardently God is sought (see Psalms 15 and 24; Amos 5:4–7, 21–24).

Contemporary appropriations of Deuteronomy 12 encounter many of the same problems that we have seen in discussing chapters 2 and 7. Vandalizing local religious shrines that do not conform to the majority religion (a synagogue or a mosque or a Zen meditation center) is hardly an action we want to tolerate in a pluralistic society. The warning about being seduced into worshiping other gods will be more along the lines of succumbing to values incompatible with the gospel that I have sketched in the discussion of the First Commandment. Thus the contemporary significance of this chapter will probably have more to do with the theology of the name of God and the central sanctuary.

We have an almost unavoidable tendency to identify holiness with a particular geographical spot or building, as if the holiness is inherent to that space and not, like the holiness of the people, derived from the presence of the Holy One. Anyone who has seen a church building destroyed by fire, or has had to vacate a church building, knows how holiness can become attached to a particular place. Yet the church is even less space-centered than the sanctuary of ancient Israel. One church in my town has a sign that says, "Meeting Place of the Church of the Redeemer." I assume that the people who composed these words recognized that the church is not the building, but the people who meet with each other *in the name of* the Redeemer. The revival movement of the nineteenth century gave us the term "camp meeting," describing services held in tents that moved from one location to another. In a sense, every meeting with God in worship is a camp meeting, in that God's presence is not fixed but given, not attached to a place but granted to a people.

To be a Christian is to be a person who is a member of those who are "called out" (*ekklesia*) and named "Christian," "belonging to Christ." The Gospel of John continues Deuteronomy's understanding of God's "habitation" ("tenting") when it designates Christ as the one in whom God "tented among us" (1:14; author's translation). Every time we gather in

Christ's name, in the place where he chooses to be present, we reaffirm our spiritual identity; and if we worship rightly, we also thereby keep apart from the Joneses (see above, chapter 4). Similarly, every time we give food to the hungry in a soup kitchen, or engage in some other act of justice, then Christ is also present (see Matt. 25:31–40 and below, chapter 12).

A NOTE ON DEUTERONOMY 13 AND 14

The danger of being seduced into the worship of other gods that forms the framework of Deuteronomy 12 continues in chapter 13, which details various situations of such seduction.

In chapter 14, Israel's holiness (v. 2) entails abstention from specific alien cultic practices (vv. 1, 21b) and from various kinds of foods—the "kosher" laws (vv. 3–21a).

While the dietary regulations are often associated with hygiene (for example, abstention from eating pork to avoid trichinosis), they are more likely not a scientific but a symbolic system. Some foods are apparently forbidden ("abhorrent thing," 14:3; "unclean," v. 10) because they seemed to ancient Israelites to be unnatural. For example, clams, oysters, lobster, crabs, and shrimp are forbidden because, unlike fish (the stereotypical seafood), they do not have fins and scales (vv. 9–10). Elsewhere, such systematic differentiation between what is considered natural and unnatural includes clothing (22:5, 11), agriculture (22:9–10), and, especially, bodily secretions (23:10–14). The book of Leviticus contains more extensive regulations regarding "uncleanness," especially with regard to sexual matters and diseases (see Leviticus 11—15, 18).

Contemporary appropriations of such biblical regulations must qualify them in the light of the New Testament critique of their role in first-century Judaism and Christianity (see Mark 7:14–23; Rom. 14; 1 Cor. 8), as well as in the light of what modern science tells us is natural and unnatural. The story of Peter's vision of the clean and unclean animals, and his resultant acceptance of Gentiles into the early church (Acts 10), could serve as a model for contemporary discussions.

The rest of Deuteronomy 14 concerns the annual and triennial tithes of produce (vv. 22–29). Like chapter 15, these regulations are economic in that they govern issues of ownership and distribution of goods (see the discussion under the commandment against stealing in chapter 5, above, [pages 85–86] and below in chapter 11, pages 127–128).

10. Economics of the Covenant Community

Deuteronomy 15:1–23; 16:1–17;
16:21–17:7

THE YEAR OF RELEASE
Deuteronomy 15:1–11

15:1 **Every seventh year you shall grant a remission of debts. ² And this is the manner of the remission: every creditor shall remit the claim that is held against a neighbor, not exacting it of a neighbor who is a member of the community, because the LORD's remission has been proclaimed. ³ Of a foreigner you may exact it, but you must remit your claim on whatever any member of your community owes you. ⁴ There will, however, be no one in need among you, because the LORD is sure to bless you in the land that the LORD your God is giving you as a possession to occupy, ⁵ if only you will obey the LORD your God by diligently observing this entire commandment that I command you today. ⁶ When the LORD your God has blessed you, as he promised you, you will lend to many nations, but you will not borrow; you will rule over many nations, but they will not rule over you.**

⁷ If there is among you anyone in need, a member of your community in any of your towns within the land that the LORD your God is giving you, do not be hard-hearted or tight-fisted toward your needy neighbor. ⁸ You should rather open your hand, willingly lending enough to meet the need, whatever it may be. ⁹ Be careful that you do not entertain a mean thought, thinking, "The seventh year, the year of remission, is near," and therefore view your needy neighbor with hostility and give nothing; your neighbor might cry to the LORD against you, and you would incur guilt. ¹⁰ Give liberally and be ungrudging when you do so, for on this account the LORD your God will bless you in all your work and in all that you undertake. ¹¹ Since there will never cease to be some in need on the earth, I therefore command you, "Open your hand to the poor and needy neighbor in your land."

The National Museum of American History in Washington, D.C., has an exhibit called "Field to Factory." The display chronicles the migration of African Americans from the agricultural fields of the South to the

industrial factories of the North, from the end of the Civil War into the
middle of the twentieth century. One of the most gripping scenes in this
exhibit depicts the life of a typical sharecropper in the South. Old pho-
tographs show the pitiful shack that masquerades as a house, barefoot children dressed in rags, and the vast fields that these people worked to earn
their share of the harvest. For many, that share never seemed to be enough
to ensure economic independence. Thus the sharecroppers remained vir-
tual slaves to the wealthy white landowners, long after the Emancipation
Proclamation. One of the quotations from a sharecropper's childhood experience illustrates the vicious cycle of poverty and exploitation:

> We went barefooted. My feet been frostbitten a lot of times. My dad couldn't
> afford to buy no shoes. He'd get in debt and he'd figure every year he was go-
> ing to get out . . . they'd tell you, "you bought so and so," they get through fig-
> uring it up you lacking a hundred dollars coming clear. What the hell could
> you do? You living on his place, you couldn't walk off.

Such sharecroppers could sing with authenticity the line from the song
"Sixteen Tons": "I owe my soul to the company store." Their plight il-
lustrates the socioeconomic problems addressed by the ancient laws in
Deuteronomy 15.

The three sets of law in Deuteronomy 15 govern debts (vv. 1–11), indentured servants (vv. 12–18), and sacrifice of animal firstlings (vv. 19–23).
Although at first glance the inclusion of the third may not seem to fit, all
three laws concern economic dimensions of the covenant community.
Our word "economy" derives from two Greek words meaning "rules [or
laws] of the household." Deuteronomy 15 contains some basic rules of
God's household. All three sets of laws are rooted theologically in the sovereignty of Israel's God over all aspects of the community's life. All demand that the people must release a claim—on money, on other people,
and on property—because all these economic assets are not "possessions,"
but ultimately come under God's lordship. To the sharecropper's com-
ment, "you living on his [the white owner's] place," the Deuteronomist
would disagree most strenuously with the implicit concept of private ownership. For the Deuteronomist, *both* of them—the sharecropper and the
owner—were living on *the Lord's* place, and this notion of divine ownership relativized all human claims (see 8:17–18).

The first two of these laws—those concerning debts and servants—are
related to far older legislation from other ancient Near Eastern cultures,
like the laws of Hammurabi, around 1700 B.C.E.; the third, regarding an-

imal sacrifice, probably reflects customs of taboo even more ancient. Yet, as we shall see, the spirit of these laws—including their economic connection—continues into the New Testament and, indeed, into contemporary contractual and liturgical customs.

The "year of release" appears to be an extension of earlier traditions concerning a "sabbath" year for the land. In the latter, it is exclusively the land, that is, agricultural land, that is "released" from its normal use. The land's sabbath may originally have been simply a recognition of its sacred character and of God's ownership (compare Lev. 25:1–5 and Deut. 15:23), but already in Exodus 23:10–11 the purpose of the release shifts to the control over the *produce* of the land: What comes up on its own while lying fallow belongs to the poor.

In Deuteronomy 15:1–11 the custom of a sabbath year release is extended to include the payment of debts. "Every seventh year [sic] . . . every creditor [literally, 'lord of a loan of his hand'] shall remit the claim that is held against his neighbor: (vv. 1–2, RSV). The word translated "remit" means literally "to let drop." The law appears to require a permanent cancellation of the debt rather than a temporary reprieve. The law thus represents a radical adaptation of an agricultural custom to an economic policy.

The intended result of the law is clear: There will be no poor (vv. 4–5). In addition, the balance of trade will be favorable (v. 6). It is not so much that poverty would be eradicated by the year of release but that following the *spirit* of the law would prevent poverty. Thus the law goes on to demand not only specific actions regarding loans but also a communal attitude of generosity. "If there *is* among you anyone in need . . . you should open your hand, willingly lending enough to meet the need, whatever it may be" (vv. 7, 8). The release of one's grip on the debtor finds its parallel in the open hand to the poor. Indeed, the law is concerned not only with outward actions but also with inner attitudes. It seeks to motivate as well as to legislate, to instill compassion as well as obedience. It speaks to the "heart" (vv. 7, 9, 10) as well as to the will (see 6:4–5; 8:17).

The authors are not, however, naïve. They recognize how easily one could decide not to make a loan when the year of release is drawing near (15:9). Why make a loan if in six months it will be cancelled? The law forbids such refusals based on self-interest and even requires that the loan be made ungrudgingly in such situations. Only those who are willing to release their grip on their neighbors will be able to open their hands to receive the blessings of God (v.10).

INDENTURED SERVANTS
Deuteronomy 15:12–18

> 15:12 **If a member of your community, whether a Hebrew man or a Hebrew woman, is sold to you and works for you six years, in the seventh year you shall set that person free.** [13] **And when you send a male slave out from you a free person, you shall not send him out empty-handed.** [14] **Provide liberally out of your flock, your threshing floor, and your wine press, thus giving to him some of the bounty with which the LORD your God has blessed you.** [15] **Remember that you were a slave in the land of Egypt, and the LORD your God redeemed you; for this reason I lay this command upon you today.** [16] **But if he says to you, "I will not go out from you," because he loves you and your household, since he is well off with you,** [17] **then you shall take an awl and thrust it through his earlobe into the door, and he shall be your slave forever. You shall do the same with regard to your female slave.** [18] **Do not consider it a hardship when you send them out from you free persons, because for six years they have given you services worth the wages of hired laborers; and the LORD your God will bless you in all that you do.**

The reality of poverty is reflected in the preceding law governing indentured servants. These people are not "slaves" in the usual sense of that term, but people who, because of economic circumstances, are pressed into becoming servants. In the ancient world, such service was often the last resort before starvation. People in economic difficulty would sell themselves or even their children as servants, thus securing at least room and board. This law protects them from *becoming* slaves. That is, it limits the duration of service to six years, after which the servant must be set free unless he or she voluntarily opts to remain in service permanently (vv. 16–17).

Comparison with the earlier form of this law in Exodus 21:2–11 reveals significant changes. There a wife provided by the household "master," along with the couple's children, must remain with the master when the servant departs. There a female servant does not enjoy the right of leaving. In Deuteronomy, the word "master" is omitted and the absence of the spouse clause suggests that the family may leave with the servant. More explicitly, female servants are included within the legislation from the outset (Deut. 15:12, 17b). Moreover, the Deuteronomic version demands the provision of basic necessities to departing servants, a share in the "bounty" that the household has received from God—including a bottle of wine (v. 14)! Indeed, as with the debt law, the legislation reaches into the inner attitude, addressing not just behavior but also how one *feels* about the behavior (v. 18).

FIRSTLINGS
Deuteronomy 15:19–23

> 15:19 **Every firstling male born of your heard and flock you shall consecrate to the LORD your God; you shall not do work with your firstling ox nor shear the firstling of your flock. ²⁰ You shall eat it, you together with your household, in the presence of the LORD your God year by year at the place that the LORD will choose. ²¹ But if it has any defect—any serious defect, such as lameness or blindness—you shall not sacrifice it to the LORD your God; ²² within your towns you may eat it, the unclean and the clean alike, as you would a gazelle or deer. ²³ Its blood, however, you must not eat; you shall pour it out on the ground like water.**

Before considering the implications of the first two laws more broadly, we turn to the law regarding firstborn male animals. These animals were to be "consecrated" to the Lord, that is, literally, "made holy." They were not to be used for ordinary economic purposes (in agriculture or for the production of clothing), but ritually sacrificed and eaten. Just as the creditor is not ultimately the "lord" over the debtor, nor the householder "master" of the servant, so individual Israelites are not ultimately owners of their animal property. Everything comes as a gift from God, and thus everything belongs to God. Sacrificing the firstborn animal is a formal recognition of the Lord's rule. Giving up this animal is functionally and symbolically equivalent to releasing debts and sending away indentured servants.

THE ECONOMY OF GOD

The laws of Deuteronmy 15 represent specific, concrete *socioeconomic* expressions of what it means to be the liberated covenant community. Here we see how and why theology and ethics are inseparable, and, indeed, why all ethics is social ethics. Here we see why the community's moral character is a product of its narrative identity.

The connections are most explicit in the second law: "Remember that you were a slave in the land of Egypt, and the Lord your God redeemed you; for this reason I lay this command upon you today" (v.15). The people liberated by the exodus are enjoined to extend the same liberation to the unfortunate within their midst, those whose debts might threaten to destroy them, and those whom poverty might force into slavery. Releasing debtors and indentured servants are the ethical actions consistent with Israel's memory of its own release from Egyptian bondage.

The other laws hint of such a connection as well. Failure to release debtors will result in their "cry to the Lord" (v. 9), reminding us of Israel's cry in a similar plight (Exod. 2:23; 3:7, 9); and sacrificing the "firstborn" animal reflects Israel's identity as *God's* firstborn (Exod. 4:21–23; 11:1–12: 50).

The Deuteronomic law did not remain the final development in the concept of a sabbatical release. Legislation in Leviticus 25 (most likely from a time later than Deuteronomy) adds a year of "jubilee" every fifty years. The indentured servant law in Leviticus 25 explicitly forbids making fellow Israelites "serve as slaves"; however, these Israelite laborers are not released until the jubilee year (vv. 39–43). The jubilee also includes the return of real property to its original owners.

Leviticus 25:10 uses the phrase "proclaim liberty throughout the land." The expression "proclaim liberty" also appears in a passage in Jeremiah (34: 8–22) from the year 597 that reflects the failure of Jerusalem citizens to obey the indentured servant law. The phrase appears once more in Isaiah 61:1–2a:

> The Spirit of the Lord God is upon me,
> because the Lord has anointed me;
> he has sent me to bring good news to the oppressed,
>   to bind up the brokenhearted,
>   to proclaim liberty to the captives,
>   and release to the prisoners;
> to proclaim the year of the LORD's favor . . .

This passage envisions the imminent arrival of God's rule, an expectation clearly in mind when Jesus quotes the passage at the outset of his ministry, according to Luke 4:16–21.

Thus a long history of tradition runs from the Mosaic law of sabbatical release to the prophets and then into the preaching of Jesus. The Greek Bible used the word *aphesis* for the Hebrew words "release" (Deut. 15:1) and "liberty" (Lev. 25:10; Jer. 34:8; Isa. 61:1), and to designate the jubilee year in Leviticus 25:28. This word appears twice in Luke 4:18 (translated "release" and "liberty"). Given the background of this language, Jesus' proclamation of the "year of the Lord" appears to refer to more than a spiritual revival. His announcement of "release" for captives would have extended to those who were captive to exploitative economic systems. Indeed, some scholars have suggested that Jesus was proclaiming an actual jubilee year, with all the radical socioeconomic consequences of that institution.

Our contemporary appropriation of the ancient laws in Deuteronomy 15 and the related texts does not depend on the extent to which these institutions were actually practiced (a moot point, in and of itself). It also does not depend on whether these laws could be followed literally today. One can imagine the outcry if Congress attempted to adopt the law on release of debts every seven years!

Nonetheless, we should not ignore the theological implications of these traditions, above all, the recognition that economic systems—how property and work and money are distributed within a society—are matters of deep theological concern. If asked for a definition of theology, few of us would probably include such matters as mortgages, interest rates, minimum wage, debts, and charge cards. Yet a contemporary Deuteronomist would have a place for such topics in a newly revised Torah.

Christians who might otherwise escape considering the texts we have discussed, and their theological challenge, would do well to reconsider another text that they almost certainly repeat frequently—the Lord's Prayer. This prayer includes a petition based on an equation. In Matthew's version it reads, "And forgive [*aphes*, 'release'] us our debts, as we forgive our debtors" (Matt. 6:12). Matthew then reiterates the conditional nature of this "release" in a subsequent verse after the prayer using "trespasses" (literally, "failures"; Matt. 6:14). Luke's version combined two different words: "forgive us our *sins*, for we ourselves forgive every one who is *indebted* to us" (Luke 11:4).

Again, given the history of traditions behind the language of "release" and "debts," it is unlikely that this part of the prayer refers only to spiritual matters; rather, it is altogether probable that "debtors" can refer to economic matters as well. The prayer asks God to treat our failures the way we treat those indebted to us. That may well be a dangerous request! Jesus' parable of the unforgiving servant (Matt. 18:23–35) illustrates the peril of this prayer better than any discursive analysis.

To conclude, the "year of release" can be traced from its roots in ancient Israelite law down to the recitation of the Lord's Prayer in almost every contemporary service of worship. The importance of the texts that convey this tradition lies not in their literal application so much as in the way they challenge us to consider our individual and corporate identity. Is that identity shaped more by the values of the covenant community or by the values of a commercial culture? Is it covenant theology or capitalist ideology that leads us almost instinctively to dismiss the "year of release" as impractical and utopian? Do contemporary readers of Deuteronomy 15 identify with the poor, or with the wealthy (the "master" of the house, the holder of the loan)? Is the story that shapes our moral character one of gratitude for liberation and God's beneficence (15:14–15), or one of self-sufficiency and individual success (8:17)? Can we with integrity ask God to release us from our spiritual sins if our economic systems hold people in the grip of poverty?

According to the cultural economy, the sharecropper with whom we began this chapter was "financially insolvent"; but, within the economy of God, the *system* that produced that insolvency was morally bankrupt. One suspects that the sharecropper would have welcomed the legislation of Deuteronomy 15 as an answer to *his* cry to God. The landowner would probably have condemned the legislation as subversive. The text challenges us to ask how the economic systems of our own time measure up to the "great society" of God's realm.

A NOTE ON DEUTERONOMY 16:1–17
AND 16:21–17:7

Deuteronomy 16:1–17 deals with the three annual festivals and 16:21–17:7 with additional regulations regarding illicit liturgical practices. (I discuss Deut. 16:18–20 in chapter 11, below.)

When we recall that there was probably no regular sabbath worship until after the exile, the three annual festivals assume even greater importance as conveyors of a religious heritage. Deuteronomy uses the traditional festivals as media for the central theological themes of the book: remembering the affliction of Egypt while living in the land of promise (16:3, 6, 12); worshiping only at the place chosen by God (vv. 2, 6, 11, 15); sharing God's blessing with others, especially the vulnerable (vv. 11, 14–17b); and—above all—enjoyment. Worship in the good land with all of its bounties calls for "rejoicing" (vv. 11, 14). Indeed, the people are to be "filled with joy" (v. 15, Jerusalem Bible). These themes have appeared already (for example, Deuteronomy 8; see chapter 6, above), and will appear again (see the discussion on Deuteronomy 24 and 26 in chapters 12 and 13, below).

The church would do well to note the "festive" quality of worship as it is depicted here, as well as the ways in which worship is inseparably tied to the ethical life of the community. Eating and drinking together—the most basic of human needs—are sacramental in that they are means of renewing the experience of the love of God and neighbor. Such graceful times should be "filled with joy" as well as solemnity, a combination that is equally fitting for the church's central celebration of the Eucharist.

Deuteronomy 16:21–17:7 reminds us of similar judgments against alien worship forms and the dangers of serving other gods noted in the first two of the Ten Commandments and in chapter 7; 12:1–3, 29–31; 14:1–2. Few, if any, of the specific forms mentioned here will be relevant for contemporary readers, although self-laceration (see Deut. 14:1) has been practiced by some contemporary Christians. More realistically, contemporary Christians face questions concerning the theological appropriateness of references to nature resulting from the need to develop an ecologically sensitive theology. For example, Should Christians refer to the earth as Mother, incorporate the creation stories of "primitive" peoples into their liturgies, and celebrate the spirits of trees and other natural objects? Similar questions arise from an increasing interest and involvement with other religions. What theological problems are involved when Christians practice meditation using a Hindu or Buddhist *mantra* or use a Sufi poem during worship? Such questions involving environmental theology and religious pluralism may represent contemporary analogs to the Deuteronomistic texts.

11. Judge, King, Priest, and Prophet

Deuteronomy 16:18–20; 17:14–20; 18:1–22

Deuteronomy 16:18–18:22 concerns four offices of the Israelite covenant community: judge, king, priest, and prophet. I leave aside details of the legislation (16:21–17:13) and focus on the presentation of the offices themselves. It is not the primary purpose of this material to provide detailed job descriptions. Rather, the purpose is to emphasize in each case something that is characteristic of the office and thus should serve as an example for the entire community. The intent here is to portray these four occupations as spiritual role models. Deuteronomy is interested in defining the central values and principles represented by each office. Just as Plato's *Republic* defined the offices of the ideal community according to his philosophy (rulers, guardians, craftsmen), so Deuteronomy here defines the offices of Israel according to the theology of the covenant community.

"JUSTICE AND ONLY JUSTICE"
Deuteronomy 16:18–20

> 16:18 **You shall appoint judges and officials throughout your tribes, in all your towns that the LORD your God is giving you, and they shall render just decisions for the people.** [19] **You must not distort justice; you must not show partiality; and you must not accept bribes, for a bribe blinds the eyes of the wise and subverts the cause of those who are in the right.** [20] **Justice, and only justice, you shall pursue, so that you may live and occupy the land that the LORD your God is giving you.**

In the Israelite justice system, most cases would be tried by citizens at the city gate (Deut. 17:5a; see above, chapter 5, page 87). Difficult cases would be taken to a regional location where a judge or Levitical priest would make the decision (17:8–13). But the primary focus here is on the character of the judges as described in the opening verses (16:18–20). The judges must be impeccably honest and impartial, unwilling to be corrupted by bribes. In short, the judges represent perhaps the most important communal value in the entire legislation of chapters 12—26: justice. "Justice, and only justice, you shall pursue." The maintenance of justice is the very life of the covenant community, as the typical Deuteronomic motivation in 16:20b suggests.

Once again, the author has Moses warn of possibilities that became realities. The prophetic books attest amply to situations in which other values (primarily power and greed) smothered the cause of justice. The wealthy imposed statutes that exploited poor people, widows, and orphans (Isa. 10:1–2; Mic. 2:1–2); people accepted bribes and shoved away the needy from the gate (Amos 5:15); those who spoke the truth in court were publicly despised (Amos 5:10). Although justice was the most important of God's requirements (Amos 5:24; Mic. 6:8; compare Deut. 10:12), instead of justice there was bloodshed (Isa. 5:7) and poison (Amos 6:12).

For Deuteronomy, the denial of justice was the ethical equivalent of the theological offense of worshiping other gods. The corruption of the court system—in which justice is available only for those who can pay for it, or are willing to commit perjury, or to accept a bribe—was a breach of covenant on the human side that often resulted from a rejection of the Lord as the "power of powers."

"Justice, and only justice, you shall pursue, so that you may live and occupy the land that the LORD your God is giving you." Any society that drops this demand from the top of its priority list ceases to be a "great society." Inequities in the American justice system have existed for years: white-collar crimes committed with relative impunity, higher conviction rates for racial minorities, adequate legal defense only for the wealthy. Even the widespread *perception* of such inequities raises serious questions. The American pledge of allegiance concludes with the words "justice for all." Given the important part that the covenant theology of the Old Testament has played in the development of American history, we would do well to ask if our pledge continues to reflect justice pursued or in fact ignores justice denied.

THE THEOLOGIAN KING
Deuteronomy 17:14–20

> 17:14 **When you have come into the land that the LORD your God is giving you, and have taken possession of it and settled in it, and you say, "I will set**

a king over me, like all the nations that are around me," [15] you may indeed set over you a king whom the LORD your God will choose. One of your own community you may set as king over you; you are not permitted to put a foreigner over you, who is not of your own community. [16] Even so, he must not acquire many horses for himself, or return the people to Egypt in order to acquire more horses, since the LORD has said to you, "You must never return that way again." [17] And he must not acquire many wives for himself, or else his heart will turn away; also silver and gold he must not acquire in great quantity for himself. [18] When he has taken the throne of his kingdom, he shall have a copy of this law written for him in the presence of the levitical priests. [19] It shall remain with him and he shall read in it all the days of his life, so that he may learn to fear the LORD his God, diligently observing all the words of this law and these statutes, [20] neither exalting himself above other members of the community nor turning aside from the commandment, either to the right or to the left, so that he and his descendants may reign over his kingdom in Israel.

Plato called for a "philosopher king" as the supreme ruler of his republic. Deuteronomy calls for a "theologian king" as the human ruler of the covenant community of Israel. The rise of the monarchy in Israel was fraught with theological as well as political problems. In the ancient Near East there was no such thing as a secular monarch. Every king was connected with a religious tradition—indeed, was often the embodiment of that tradition (for example, the pharaoh in Egypt). Some cultures considered royalty to be divine, or at least far above ordinary human subjects. Some royal enthusiasts within ancient Israel harbored similar thoughts about their king (see Psalm 89:26–27). Such notions of royalty led easily to the abuse of power. While kings were understood as the chief executors of justice (see Psalm 72), often the temptations of power led to *in*justice. A classic case is the incident of Naboth's vineyard, in which royal power was used to bribe false witnesses, producing an unjust death sentence and the extortion of property (1 Kings 21).

Deuteronomy was well aware of the difference between the ideal and the real monarch. Indeed, much of the Deuteronomistic History focuses on the problems of human kingship both in principle and in practice. Deuteronomy 17:14–20 warns of the abuses of power that the author knew all too well as accurate history. The specific prohibitions are especially reminiscent of the reign of Solomon, perhaps because he more than Saul and even David appears to have established the monarchy in ways similar to other contemporary regimes. Although the king is not to "acquire many horses" (v. 16), Solomon had "forty thousand stalls of horses for his chariots, and twelve thousand horsemen" (1 Kings 4:26)—what we would call a "military-industrial complex." Although the king was not to "acquire many wives" (Deut. 17:17), Solomon did so—some of them certainly foreigners and therefore all the more likely to want their own religious shrines and to turn the heart of the king away from the Lord (compare Deut. 17:17a and 1 Kings 11:4–8). Although the king was not to acquire silver and gold "in great quantity" (Deut. 17:17b), Solomon amassed a fortune of legendary proportions (1 Kings 10:14–22). In general, compare 1 Samuel 8 and 12; 2 Samuel 7.

These admonitions of Deuteronomy thus call for a ruler whose lifestyle is not marked by unbridled military power, excessive and compromising foreign relations, or unchecked wealth. Moreover, Deuteronomy implies that hereditary succession is inconsistent with covenant theology, for the king is to be the one whom *the Lord* will choose (17:15). Continuation of a dynasty depends on covenant obedience (v. 20b), a condition that poses a serious qualification to ideas of an "everlasting covenant" (for instance, 2 Sam. 7:14–17; 23:5; contrast Psalm 132:12). Probably the text has in mind the ideal of an appointment mediated through God's spokespersons, the prophets, appropriately called "king makers and king breakers." Indeed, the monarchy began with Saul and David being anointed by Samuel, an institution quickly abandoned with the succession of Solomon (see 1 Kings 1:35) but revived sporadically (as with Elijah, 1 Kings 19:15–16).

The question of the selection of a ruler goes to the heart of covenant theology. Since the Lord is Israel's suzerain (the "Great King" in treaty language), how can there be a human king (see 1 Sam. 12:12)? Yet the reality of political organization and national security at times seems to demand such a figure (see again 1 Sam. 8). Deuteronomy recognizes the reality, but holds out for the *ideal* ruler.

What, then, is the ideal ruler? He is a student of the Torah (Deut. 17:18–20). The first thing he is to do after his inauguration is to "have a copy of this law written for him" and he is to study it every day of his life. While the text does not specify what "this law" refers to, it probably includes the entire book of Deuteronomy (see 1:5). The king is to be both an avid reader and a diligent observer of the law. In our society, it would be something like a combination of the chief scholar of the Constitution and its chief executor. In this way, the ruler will not "exalt himself above other members of the community." Far from being above the law, the ruler is a student *of* the law, and its most important public representative. In fact, he will be the primary role model for learning and teaching (see 6:4–9).

The great society is based on the great commandment, and the truly great ruler will be one who recognizes the sovereignty of the Lord and the rule of the law. The portrait of the ideal king here is related to what the Deuteronomic school hoped would be the normal pattern (see 1 Kings 2:3–4). With a few exceptions, that hope was not realized, but it remains worth consideration by any society. In our own recent history, the Watergate crisis raised similar questions about presidential authority and the rule of the law. One of the convicted conspirators has commented, "Who is to say [a presidential order] is illegal if it's directed by the chief law enforcement officer of the land?"

If we asked in what ways most Americans think of their president as a role model, would constant study and knowledge of the country's history and constitutional traditions rank above power, wealth and prestige? Is our primary model an imperial president or a covenantal president? What image is most important for such a leader to present to the public? Is it determined by pollsters and superficial standards of popularity, or by the country's constitutional polity? Deuteronomy knew what was most important within the polity of ancient Israel, and thus challenges us to consider what is most important within our own.

FEEDING THE PREACHER
Deuteronomy 18:1–8

> 18:1 The levitical priests, the whole tribe of Levi, shall have no allotment or inheritance within Israel. They may eat the sacrifices that are the LORD's portion ² but they shall have no inheritance among the other members of the community; the LORD is their inheritance, as he promised them.
>
> ³ This shall be the priests' due from the people, from those offering a sacrifice, whether an ox or a sheep: they shall give to the priest the shoulder, the two jowls, and the stomach. ⁴ The first fruits of your grain, your wine, and your oil, as well as the first of the fleece of your sheep, you shall give him. ⁵ For the LORD your God has chosen Levi out of all your tribes, to stand and minister in the name of the LORD, him and his sons for all time.
>
> ⁶ If a Levite leaves any of your towns, from wherever he has been residing in Israel, and comes to the place that the LORD will choose (and he may come whenever he wishes), ⁷ then he may minister in the name of the LORD his God, like all his fellow-Levites who stand to minister there before the LORD. ⁸ They shall have equal portions to eat, even though they have income from the sale of family possessions.

In the South of my childhood (and still today, in some areas), it was not uncommon for the preacher to receive little monetary pay but many invitations to dinner, donations of garden produce, and an occasional country ham left at the doorstep. Deuteronomy would approve of this pastoral system, even if a modern economy makes it unsatisfactory. The legislation concerning the Levitical priests in Deuteronomy 18:1–8 tells us nothing about their ecclesiastical duties. As with the judge and even more so the king, the text gives no job description (there are ample instructions in the book of Leviticus). Instead, the text focuses on the provision of the most basic needs for the priests—food and clothing.

The Levitical priests—that is, "the whole tribe of Levi"—are unique among all the tribes in that they "have no allotment or inheritance within Israel" (18:1). They have no land, and thus no way to provide food or clothing for themselves by agriculture or by animal husbandry. Hence they are totally dependent on the rest of the community for their sustenance. In a sense, the priests are welfare recipients. They live by entitlements—donations of sacrificial offerings, first harvests, and first shearings. Yet Deuteronomy makes clear that their dependence does not make them poor, much less socially repulsive. Indeed, they are expected to share in the bounty of the land, to eat and be filled, and to rejoice in it, along with everyone else (see 12:11–12, 18–19; 14:22–29).

Deuteronomy focuses on the dependence of the Levitical priests because precisely in their dependence they hold up a mirror to the entire community. They model *Israel's* reliance on the Lord, and serve as a continual reminder of the gratitude that should follow from that reliance. In a sense, their everyday lives witness to the lesson of Deuteronomy 8:18: "it is [the Lord] who gives you power to get wealth." Thus, rather than being an object of scorn because they are on the dole, the priests should be an object of imitation because they are the recipients of grace. They must trust in the community the same way that the community must trust in the Lord. "In this way, the position of the Levite typifies that of all Israel" (McConville, *Law*, 1984, 152).

PROPHETS LIKE MOSES
Deuteronomy 18:9–22

> 18:9 **When you come into the land that the LORD your God is giving you, you must not learn to imitate the abhorrent practices of those nations.** [10] **No one shall be found among you who makes a son or daughter pass through fire, or who practices divination, or is a soothsayer, or an augur, or a sorcerer,** [11] **or one who casts spells, or who consults ghosts or spirits, or who seeks oracles from the dead.** [12] **For whoever does these things is abhorrent to the LORD; it is because of such abhorrent practices that the LORD your**

God is driving them out before you. [13] You must remain completely loyal to the LORD your God. [14] Although these nations that you are about to dispossess do give heed to soothsayers and diviners, as for you, the LORD your God does not permit you to do so.

[15] The LORD your God will raise up for you a prophet like me from among your own people; you shall heed such a prophet. [16] This is what you requested of the LORD your God at Horeb on the day of the assembly when you said: "If I hear the voice of the LORD my God any more, or ever again see this great fire, I will die." [17] Then the LORD replied to me: "They are right in what they have said. [18] I will raise up for them a prophet like you from among their own people; I will put my words in the mouth of the prophet, who shall speak to them everything that I command. [19] Anyone who does not heed the words that the prophet shall speak in my name, I myself will hold accountable. [20] But any prophet who speaks in the name of other gods, or who presumes to speak in my name a word that I have not commanded the prophet to speak—that prophet shall die." [21] You may say to yourself, "How can we recognize a word that the LORD has not spoken?" [22] If a prophet speaks in the name of the LORD but the thing does not take place or prove true, it is a word that the LORD has not spoken. The prophet has spoken it presumptuously; do not be frightened by it.

This section is held together by a concern for the proper mode of discerning God's will for the community. In the ancient Near East, there were many possible resources available for such discernment. One could examine an animal's liver, read the flight of birds, or talk to the dead through a medium (Saul tried the last with rather unpleasant results, 1 Sam. 28:8–14). The opening passage (Deut. 18:9–14) condemns any such form of inquiry. Instead, God will provide the proper medium for revelation—the prophet. The prophet is the model for spiritual discernment that is compatible with the central traditions of the covenant community. And the model for the prophet is, of course, Moses.

The text then repeats in essence the framework of Deuteronomy 5, recounting Moses' appointment as covenant mediator, but adding words that were not reported there: "I will raise up for them a prophet like you." Moses is clearly here understood as the starting point for the office of prophet, those who may preface their words with the formula "thus says the Lord."

Yet a problem immediately presents itself: How can the people know a true prophet from a false prophet? Just using the words "thus says the Lord" does not guarantee the legitimacy of a self-proclaimed prophet. This was not an idle question in Israel's history, for situations arose in which people claimed to be prophets, yet presented messages which differed radically from one another and the acceptance of which would produce radically different results (see 1 Kings 22; Jeremiah 28).

Deuteronomy offers two criteria to distinguish false from true prophecy: the false prophet (1) speaks in the name of other gods (18:20a; see 13:1–5), and (2) predicts what fails to happen (18:22). The first is easy to determine, the second problematic, because if the prophet is foretelling doom and destruction, by the time it happens it will be too late! Until the exile the genuine prophets of Israel by and large *did* foretell doom and destruction, as does much of Deuteronomy. In this sense the prophets were failures, for they were unable to convince the people of the truthfulness of their message. The result was that their dire predictions came true (see Isa. 6:9–12).

Nevertheless, the main point of Deuteronomy 18:9–22 is to hold up the prophets as the legitimate communicators of God's will. It is they who show *how* one should go about discerning what God requires and what the future holds. The prophets did that not by gazing into a crystal ball but by looking back at Israel's history—much as Moses does in Deuteronomy 1—11—and, in the light of this history, taking a hard look at Israel's current way of life. If that life conformed to the grand central story and the great commandment, then all would be well; but if it did not, then the horizon was dark—"gloom with no brightness in it" (Amos 5:20).

It is no easier for us today to discern the will of God, or to know with certainty who might be speaking God's word. But we do know that someone who holds some value higher than God is speaking falsely (see chapter 3, above), and we know that an interpretation of God's will that is incompatible with the Christian story is also likely to be questionable. That does not by any means make our discerning easy, but it does give it authoritative *guidance*, which, again, is what *torah* means.

Judge, king, priest, and prophet. Deuteronomy presents us with four offices of the covenant community. But in defining the responsibilities of these offices, the text avoids the practical and focuses on principles. It gives us in each case a model of one of the fundamental values of the community: justice (judges), learning (king), trust (priest), and truth (prophet).

A NOTE ON DEUTERONOMY 19—23; 24:1–9, 16, 19–22; AND 25:1–19

For the laws regarding homicide (19:1–13), see the discussion on murder and the Sixth Commandment in chapter 5, above. For discussions of 19:14

(removing boundaries), 24:19–22 (gleaning law), 24:7 (kidnapping), 25:13–16 (weights and measures), see my comments on stealing and the Eighth Commandment in chapter 5, above. For a discussion of 19:15–20, see the discussion on lying and the Ninth Commandment in chapter 5, above, pages 86–87.

Exemptions from military service appear in 20:1–9 (see 24:5). The policy on conquered cities (20:10–18) reminds us of chapter 7 (compare 23:3–6; 25:17–19). Several laws involve what we would call conservation (20:19–20; 22:6–7). The ritual for an unsolved murder (21:1–9) provides a good example of the communal perspective of Deuteronomy on the one hand. On the other hand, individual responsibility is stressed in 24:16 (contrast the implication of 5:9), and individual property rights are involved in 23:24–25. Several laws concern the rights of women (21:10–17; 22:13–21; 25:5–10). See the discussion on adultery and the Seventh Commandment in chapter 5, above, and 22:22–30; 24:1–4.

Cultic purity is again regulated in 22:5, 9–13; 23:1–3, 9–18; 24:8; 25:4, 11–12. Some of this material may prohibit practices popular in Canaanite culture. For some interesting contrasts here see Isaiah 56:3–5 and the story of the Ethiopian eunuch (Acts 8:26–40); see Deuteronomy 14 and the note on it in chapter 9, above. Humanitarian laws (Deut. 22:1–4; 23:15, 19–20; 24:6; 25:1–3) reflect the concerns I discuss in chapter 12, below.

12. The Cry of Justice
Deuteronomy 24:10–15, 17–18

24:10 **When you make your neighbor a loan of any kind, you shall not go into the house to take the pledge. ¹¹ You shall wait outside, while the person to whom you are making the loan brings the pledge out to you. ¹² If the person is poor, you shall not sleep in the garment given you as the pledge. ¹³ You shall give the pledge back by sunset, so that your neighbor may sleep in the cloak and bless you; and it will be to your credit before the LORD your God.**

¹⁴ You shall not withhold the wages of poor and needy laborers, whether other Israelites or aliens who reside in your land in one of your towns. ¹⁵ You shall pay them their wages daily before sunset, because they are poor and their livelihood depends on them; otherwise they might cry to the LORD against you, and you would incur guilt. . . .

¹⁷ You shall not deprive a resident alien or an orphan of justice; you shall not take a widow's garment in pledge. ¹⁸ Remember that you were a slave in Egypt and the LORD your God redeemed you from there; therefore I command you to do this.

Michael had worked hard all morning in the hot sun. He had filled his quota of a bushel of wheat sooner than he had expected, and with a sense of satisfaction and relief he had left his basket in the row and moved over to the side of the field, resting under the shade of a lone tree. Once he was rested, he would get his basket, take it to the foreman, and receive his pay. Then he would go home, happy to have his day's wages. It was hard for a migrant worker—especially an alien—to find regular work, and a day's wage might have to stretch for several day's worth of food.

As Michael was about to doze off, the foreman appeared suddenly and shouted angrily at him: "Why are you lying here in the shade when there is work to do?" Michael quickly told the foreman that he had already finished his assigned work, but the foreman would not believe him and refused to pay his wages. He even confiscated Michael's overcoat as a pawn for the foreman's share of his work.

When Michael went home and told his friends what had happened, they urged him to appeal to the local mayor. Surely he would see that justice was done. Michael was illiterate, but he found a man who could write, and had this letter sent to the mayor: "Let His Honor the mayor hear the word of his servant: your servant was reaping in the field, and had finished; and I gathered in about a bushel before my rest. When I had finished reaping, there came Hashabiah the son of Shobai, and he took your servant's overcoat. And all of my fellows will witness on my behalf, they who reap with me in the heat of the sun, my fellows will witness on my behalf that truly I am free of guilt. Restore my overcoat. Do not leave me helpless."

(Adapted from the Hashavyehu Ostracon, Naveh.)

THE HEART OF THE LAW

We do not know what happened to Michael, or even if that was his name, for most of the above is a fictionalized reconstruction. We do not know whether the mayor came to his help, or even if he responded to his petition. All we know is what we can guess from Michael's petition, written on a potsherd, a scrap of pottery, sometime around the year 900 B.C.E.

For many of us, this little piece of pottery, which archaeologists call an ostracon, may be nothing more than an artifact of ancient history, something for linguists to puzzle over. But that is not the way Moses or Nathan or Amos would have looked at it. They would have picked up this ostracon, shaken it in our faces, and cried, "See, *this* is what God's law is all about. This is what it was intended to correct—indeed, to *prevent*." They would have agreed with the modern author Nikos Kazantzakis, who writes, "God always works in this way. Deep in the foundations of wrong he buries the small despised cry of justice" (Kazantzakis, *Temptation*, 1960, 34).

I have chosen to discuss these laws in Deuteronomy 24 because, with chapter 15, they typify Deuteronomy's concern for justice for the vulnerable. While the details of such laws may often seem irrelevant to us, we can never dismiss their ethical substance. They are practical examples of the principle that was announced in the prologue: The love of God and the love of strangers are bound together as a single, indissoluble command (10:12–22).

The foreman in the historical incident broke all three of the laws in Deuteronomy 24:10–15, 17–18. He kept a poor man's overcoat overnight, he refused to pay wages on the day they were earned, and he thus deprived the worker of justice. The overcoat was all that a poor person had for protection from the elements. In a way similar to today's homeless street people, he would sleep in this coat during the chill Palestinian nights. For this reason, no one was to keep an overcoat as a "pledge" or pawn overnight, that is, as collateral for a loan. The creditor was required to return the overcoat at sunset for the owner to use overnight. The first part of the law (24:10) also protects a poor person's dignity and privacy, since the creditor is forbidden to enter the person's home to take a pledge. The law concludes (v. 13b) with the typical motivation clauses. Obedience will provide for the comfort of the poor person (a humanitarian motivation), will result in the poor person's invoking a blessing on the creditor (reward), and will signify the creditor's righteousness before God. The final phrase says literally, "it will be righteousness to you before the Lord your God" (RSV).

BEING RIGHT WITH GOD

Deuteronomy 24:13b, the concluding motivational phrase, is surely the most important. Ensuring justice for the disadvantaged puts one "in the right" with God. The notion here is not so much receiving "credit" (NRSV) as being recognized as living appropriately. One acts this way not to gain a reward but simply because this is the way that is fitting for one's identity. It is not merely coincidental, therefore, that the phrase at the end of verse 13 is identical to that in 6:25—"if we diligently observe this entire commandment before the LORD our God . . . we will be in the right" (NRSV). Or, as the RSV puts it, "it will be righteousness for us."

Perhaps we have become so sensitive about *self*-righteousness that we have almost lost sense of what righteousness means. It means being and acting in right relationship—here with God and with one's fellows. That the phrase "it will be righteousness for us/you" appears in Deuteronomy 6 after invoking the grand central story of Israel, and here after commanding a specific act of humanitarian compassion, underscores the correlation of story and law, exodus and Sinai (Horeb), theology and ethics.

The correlation is illustrated again in the motivations for the next two laws. The laborer whose wages are unjustly withheld may "cry to the LORD against you, and you would incur guilt" (24:15; the identical phrase occurs in 15:9). Here the cry for justice would be directed against an Israelite in much the same way that *Israel's* cry was directed against Pharaoh in Egypt (see Exod. 2:23–25; 3:7–9). To invite such a cry is to become the oppressor. In effect, it is to reverse roles in Israel's story, and to become the villain rather than the one rescued.

Thus the third law (Deut. 24:17–18) directly links the act of justice with the mental act of remembering that story: "remember that you were a slave in Egypt and the Lord your God redeemed you from there; therefore I command you to do this." In the earlier chapters, memory was primarily a theological category that rooted Israel's collective identity in the stories of the past (5:15; 7:18; 8:2, 18; 9:7). Now we see that memory is also an ethical category, for those who genuinely identify with the words "*we* were Pharaoh's slaves in Egypt" (6:21) will behave accordingly. Memory, correctly understood, produces being "right with God." Loyalty to God is the primary theological form of memory; protection of the helpless is the primary ethical form.

Acting justly means that one is not an oppressor but a liberator. One is "right with God" when one acts the way that God acts—that is, as the chief agent in the exodus story. This is perhaps the most profound implication of the law. It intends to reproduce the divine act of liberation whenever and wherever injustice appears. Salvation and redemption are not simply events in the distant past. They are present whenever Israel, as the covenant community, lives according to the grand central story. That is why the commandment that ensures an overcoat on a cold night reveals the heart of the law. For God gives the law as the political means by which God's salvation and justice may be maintained in society, even for those who are not members of the society (aliens). It is the very purpose of the law to create a community in which the exodus of the oppressed is a continuing activity.

The meaning of the law is found in the grand central story (6:20–25), but the meaning of the story is incomplete without the fulfillment of the law. The author of James speaks out of this tradition when admonishing us to be "not hearers [of the word] who forget but doers who act," because "faith by itself, if it has no works, is dead" (James 1:25; 2:17).

13. The Grand Central Story—
Reprise
Deuteronomy 26:1–19

COMING INTO THE LAND
Deuteronomy 26:1–11

26:1 **When you have come into the land that the LORD your God is giving you as an inheritance to possess, and you possess it, and settle in it, ² you shall take some of the first of all the fruit of the ground, which you harvest from the land that the LORD your God is giving you, and you shall put it in a basket and go to the place that the LORD your God will choose as a dwelling for his name. ³ You shall go to the priest who is in office at that time, and say to him, "Today I declare to the LORD your God that I have come into the land that the LORD swore to our ancestors to give us." ⁴ When the priest takes the basket from your hand and sets it down before the altar of the LORD your God, ⁵ you shall make this response before the LORD your God: "A wandering Aramean was my ancestor; he went down into Egypt and lived there as an alien, few in number, and there he became a great nation, mighty and populous. ⁶ When the Egyptians treated us harshly and afflicted us, by imposing hard labor on us, ⁷ we cried to the LORD, the God of our ancestors; the LORD heard our voice and saw our affliction, our toil, and our oppression. ⁸ The LORD brought us out of Egypt with a mighty hand and an outstretched arm, with a terrifying display of power, and with signs and wonders; ⁹ and he brought us into this place and gave us this land, a land flowing with milk and honey. ¹⁰ So now I bring the first of the fruit of the ground that you, O LORD, have given me." You shall set it down before the LORD your God and bow down before the LORD your God. ¹¹ Then you, together with the Levites and the aliens who reside among you, shall celebrate with all the bounty that the LORD your God has given to you and to your house.**

On the 4th of July a number of years ago, well ahead of the collapse of the Iron Curtain, my local newspaper ran a story about a man who had defected from East Germany thirty years before. A picture of the man sitting in his office showed a large American flag spread across the wall behind his desk, with a framed copy of the Declaration of Independence beside it. In the article, this transplanted German, now an American citizen, talked about his experience of fleeing a dictatorship and coming to the United States as if it were only yesterday. "You can't appreciate freedom," he said, "unless you've lived in a country where it doesn't exist."

Most of us have not had that experience, so if we accept this immigrant's judgment, most of us cannot appreciate the independence that we enjoy. No doubt that was why the newspaper ran the story, hoping that it would inspire us to be more grateful for where we live, and our lives would reflect that gratitude.

Some Americans, of course, would find it difficult to identify with that immigrant. Native Americans, for example, would say that their communal story does not include immigration (that is why they were *native* Americans). African Americans would insist that their ancestral immigration was a brutal exile *from* freedom *to* oppression. Many Americans who have been here for generations cannot identify with *any* story about coming into the land. Yet everyone who lives in North or South America derives ultimately from an immigrant.

The author of Deuteronomy would certainly have no problem identifying with the immigrant's story. In fact, the purpose of the conclusion to Moses' second address in chapter 26 is to prescribe a liturgical recognition of the immigrant status of *all* Israelites, of the consequent responsibility for others, and finally of the people's covenant agreement on which their tenure of the land depends. Legislation for firstfruits and the third year tithe have already appeared in Deuteronomy (12:17; 14:22–27 and 14:28–29, respectively) and elsewhere (Exod. 23:19; 34:26; Lev. 23:9–14; Num. 18:12–13). So it is clear that the *symbolic* meaning of these rituals here in Deuteronomy 26 is paramount. Indeed, with such urgency does Deuteronomy view the occupation of the land that this ritual replaces the centrality of the festival of Passover.

The firstfruits ritual (26:1–11) celebrates the first agricultural produce of the year. It is possible that the author has in mind a once-for-all ceremony to be observed by the first generation of immigrants only. But it is more likely that an annual ritual for all generations is here prescribed, or at least that the traditional firstfruits liturgy is now charged with the historical significance of entering the land. If so, the ritual is something like a spring Thanksgiving service in which everyone is required to play the role of settler. Everyone has to pretend that they are that generation (Moses' audience) who first came into the land. When they bring the basket of produce to the priest at the central sanctuary, they have a "responsive reading" to say to the priest: "Today I declare to the Lord your God that I have come into the land that the Lord swore to our ancestors to give us." The liturgy forces the participants to identify with the immigrants through their imagination.

In the present time of worship, the participants (who are in the future of the text) are fused with the past. They reenact the entrance into the land, and thus they are induced to experience that gratitude for the land that only those who had escaped Egypt and crossed the wilderness could really know. That gratitude is the chief affection to be stimulated is apparent in that the word "give" is used to refer to the land six times within verses 1–3 and 9–11, and in both rituals the goodness of the land is referred to as "flowing with milk and honey" (vv. 9 and 15; see 6:3).

The declaration "I have come into the land" (26:3) is thus an autobiographical fiction played out within the drama of worship. The ritual is literally a rite of passage that celebrates coming into the promised land. But entrance into the land is only one part of Israel's grand central story, and remembering this part alone is necessary but not sufficient for complete Israelite identity. Therefore, the worshiper is required to recite the entire story, beginning with Jacob, "a wandering [or perhaps 'perishing'] Aramean," who emigrated from Canaan and lived "as an alien" in Egypt, was there oppressed, brought out by God with wonderful power, and finally led to "this place." When the worshiper then says, "so now I bring the first of the fruit," the narrative recitation has shifted from the third person singular ("he") to the first person plural ("we") to the first person singular ("I"). The process of corporate identification is complete, and the contemporary worshiper has become the alien immigrant of the past, rejoicing in the gift of the land as if he or she *is* one of the first generation.

GRATITUDE AND GENEROSITY
Deuteronomy 26:12–15

> 26:12 When you have finished paying all the tithe of your produce in the third year (which is the year of the tithe), giving it to the Levites, the aliens, the orphans, and the widows, so that they may eat their fill within your towns, 13 then you shall say before the LORD your God: "I have removed the sacred portion from the house, and I have given it to the Levites, the resident aliens, the orphans, and the widows, in accordance with your entire commandment that you commanded me; I have neither transgressed nor forgotten any of your commandments: 14 I have not eaten of it while in mourning; I have not removed any of it while I was unclean; and I have not offered any of it to the dead. I have obeyed the LORD my God, doing just as

you commanded me. ¹⁵ Look down from your holy habitation, from heaven, and bless your people Israel and the ground that you have given us, as you swore to our ancestors—a land flowing with milk and honey."

For Deuteronomy, gratitude, like love, has a dual orientation. It is the basis for worship—for allegiance to the Lord alone—and it is the basis for stewardship—for equitable distribution of the bounty of the land. This duality appears at the end of the firstfruits liturgy (v. 10), where the participant is instructed to "bow down before the Lord your God"—literally an act of physical prostration—and then in the next verse is called "*with* the Levites and the aliens who reside among you" to "celebrate with all the bounty that the Lord your God has given to you" (v. 11). Again, just as remembering the story is the basis for the great commandment (see 6:20–25), so it is the basis for the great society.

The horizontal dimension of gratitude becomes the focus of the third year tithe ritual (vv. 26:12–15), another repetition from the festival calendar (14:28–29). Here the beneficiaries are listed twice for emphasis (26:12, 13), and everyone is to eat and be full (v. 12b; see 8:10, 12). The relinquishment of produce for their benefit is linked to the holiness of the worshiper by a negative declaration concerning alien cult practices (v. 14), thus connecting Israel's holiness to the Lord with charity to the poor (see 14:2).

Thus the two liturgies here at the conclusion of the "statutes and ordinances" remind us of the dual focus in the introduction to this section in 10:12–21, where the love of the Lord was coupled with the love of the alien. The liturgical sections then close with a prayer recognizing God's transcendent sovereignty and asking for God's continued blessing, a final acknowledgment that the "land flowing with milk and honey" derives from the Lord alone (26:15).

The liturgies in chapter 26 therefore provide a fitting reminder of the central concerns of Deuteronomy—the great commandment, the grand central story, and the great society. The "statutes and ordinances" are now concluded, and Moses, again acting as mediator, summarizes the formal agreement between the two parties of the covenant, the Lord and Israel, in 26:16–19.

THE TREATY CONCLUDES
Deuteronomy 26:16–19

26:16 **This very day the LORD your God is commanding you to observe these statutes and ordinances; so observe them diligently with all your heart and** with all your soul. [17] **Today you have obtained the LORD's agreement: to be your God; and for you to walk in his ways, to keep his statutes, his commandments, and his ordinances, and to obey him. [18] Today the LORD has obtained your agreement: to be his treasured people, as he promised you, and to keep his commandments; [19] for him to set you high above all nations that he has made, in praise and in fame and in honor; and for you to be a people holy to the LORD your God, as he promised.**

The Lord will be their God, and they will be the Lord's people. This is the most basic formulation of the treaty between them. Especially in the prophetic books of the Old Testament, the motif "my people" appears repeatedly to indicate either the renunciation or reaffirmation of the covenant relationship (renunciation by God: Hos. 1:8–9; by Israel: Jer. 2:26–32; reaffirmation by God: Isa. 40:1; Jer. 30:22; Ezek. 11:20). Also, the New Testament appropriates the language of "God's own people" to describe the church (1 Pet. 2:9–10). Here in Deuteronomy 26:16–19, the declaration of Israel as the people of the Lord functions as both conclusion to the stipulations of the treaty (Deuteronomy 12—26) and transition to the completion of the covenant-making process in the remaining chapters.

14. Showers of Blessing, Droughts of Curse
Deuteronomy 27:1–30:20

Deuteronomy 27 continues the formal process of covenant making that concluded chapter 26. Once the people have entered the land, the "words of this law" are to be inscribed at a public place to serve as a constant reminder, and the people are to build a sacrificial altar for "rejoicing before the Lord." Moses then declares Israel to be "the people of the Lord" (27:9; see 26:17–19) and, again looking toward the future, instructs the Levites that, on arriving in the land, they are to proclaim a series of curses as punishments for failure to keep the covenant. This series of curses is then followed by a much longer list of blessings and curses in chapter 28, pronounced immediately by Moses.

REALPOLITIK
Deuteronomy 28:1–68

28:1 If you will only obey the LORD your God, by diligently observing all his commandments that I am commanding you today, the LORD your God will set you high above all the nations of the earth; ² all these blessings shall come upon you and overtake you, if you obey the LORD your God:

³ Blessed shall you be in the city, and blessed shall you be in the field.

⁴ Blessed shall be the fruit of your womb, the fruit of your ground, and the fruit of your livestock, both the increase of your cattle and the issue of your flock.

⁵ Blessed shall be your basket and your kneading bowl.

⁶ Blessed shall you be when you come in, and blessed shall you be when you go out.

⁷ The LORD will cause your enemies who rise against you to be defeated before you; they shall come out against you one way, and flee before you seven ways. ⁸ The LORD will command the blessing upon you in your barns, and in all that you undertake; he will bless you in the land that the LORD

your God is giving you. [9] The LORD will establish you as his holy people, as he has sworn to you, if you keep the commandments of the LORD your God and walk in his ways. [10] All the peoples of the earth shall see that you are called by the name of the LORD, and they shall be afraid of you. [11] The LORD will make you abound in prosperity, in the fruit of your womb, in the fruit of your livestock, and in the fruit of your ground in the land that the LORD swore to your ancestors to give you. [12] The LORD will open for you his rich storehouse, the heavens, to give the rain of your land in its season and to bless all your undertakings. You will lend to many nations, but you will not borrow. [13] The LORD will make you the head, and not the tail; you shall be only at the top, and not at the bottom—if you obey the commandments of the LORD your God, which I am commanding you today, by diligently observing them, [14] and if you do not turn aside from any of the words that I am commanding you today, either to the right or to the left, following other gods to serve them.

[15] But if you will not obey the LORD your God by diligently observing all his commandments and decrees, which I am commanding you today, then all these curses shall come upon you and overtake you:

[16] Cursed shall you be in the city, and cursed shall you be in the field.

[17] Cursed shall be your basket and your kneading bowl.

[18] Cursed shall be the fruit of your womb, the fruit of your ground, the increase of your cattle and the issue of your flock.

[19] Cursed shall you be when you come in, and cursed shall you be when you go out.

[20] The LORD will send upon you disaster, panic, and frustration in everything you attempt to do, until you are destroyed and perish quickly, on account of the evil of your deeds, because you have forsaken me. [21] The LORD will make the pestilence cling to you until it has consumed you off the land that you are entering to possess. [22] The LORD will afflict you with consumption, fever, inflammation, with fiery heat and drought, and with blight and mildew; they shall pursue you until you perish. [23] The sky over your head shall be bronze, and the earth under you iron. [24] The LORD will change the rain of your land into powder, and only dust shall come down upon you from the sky until you are destroyed.

[25] The LORD will cause you to be defeated before your enemies; you shall go out against them one way and flee before them seven ways. You shall become an object of horror to all the kingdoms of the earth. [26] Your corpses shall be food for every bird of the air and animal of the earth, and there shall be no one to frighten them away.

[27] The LORD will afflict you with the boils of Egypt, with ulcers, scurvy, and itch, of which you cannot be healed.

[28] The LORD will afflict you with madness, blindness, and confusion of mind; [29] you shall grope about at noon as blind people grope in darkness, but you shall be unable to find your way; and you shall be continually abused and robbed, without anyone to help.

³⁰ You shall become engaged to a woman, but another man shall lie with her. You shall build a house, but not live in it. You shall plant a vineyard, but not enjoy its fruit. ³¹ Your ox shall be butchered before your eyes, but you shall not eat of it. Your donkey shall be stolen in front of you, and shall not be restored to you. Your sheep shall be given to your enemies, without anyone to help you. ³² Your sons and daughters shall be given to another people, while you look on; you will strain your eyes looking for them all day but be powerless to do anything. ³³ A people whom you do not know shall eat up the fruit of your ground and of all your labors; you shall be continually abused and crushed, ³⁴ and driven mad by the sight that your eyes shall see.

³⁵ The LORD will strike you on the knees and on the legs with grievous boils of which you cannot be healed, from the sole of your foot to the crown of your head. ³⁶ The LORD will bring you, and the king whom you set over you, to a nation that neither you nor your ancestors have known, where you shall serve other gods, of wood and stone. ³⁷ You shall become an object of horror, a proverb, and a byword among all the peoples where the LORD will lead you.

³⁸ You shall carry much seed into the field but shall gather little in, for the locust shall consume it. ³⁹ You shall plant vineyards and dress them, but you shall neither drink the wine nor gather the grapes, for the worm shall eat them. ⁴⁰ You shall have olive trees throughout all your territory, but you shall not anoint yourself with the oil, for your olives shall drop off. ⁴¹ You shall have sons and daughters, but they shall not remain yours, for they shall go into captivity. ⁴² All your trees and the fruit of your ground the cicada shall take over. ⁴³ Aliens residing among you shall ascend above you higher and higher, while you shall descend lower and lower. ⁴⁴ They shall lend to you but you shall not lend to them; they shall be the head and you shall be the tail.

⁴⁵ All these curses shall come upon you, pursuing and overtaking you until you are destroyed, because you did not obey the LORD your God, by observing the commandments and the decrees that he commanded you. ⁴⁶ They shall be among you and your descendants as a sign and a portent forever.

⁴⁷ Because you did not serve the LORD your God joyfully and with gladness of heart for the abundance of everything, ⁴⁸ therefore you shall serve your enemies whom the LORD will send against you, in hunger and thirst, in nakedness and lack of everything. He will put an iron yoke on your neck until he has destroyed you. ⁴⁹ The LORD will bring a nation from far away, from the end of the earth, to swoop down on you like an eagle, a nation whose language you do not understand, ⁵⁰ a grim-faced nation showing no respect to the old or favor to the young. ⁵¹ It shall consume the fruit of your livestock and the fruit of your ground until you are destroyed, leaving you neither grain, wine, and oil, nor the increase of your cattle and the issue of your flock, until it has made you perish. ⁵² It shall besiege you in all your towns until your high and fortified walls, in which you trusted, come down

throughout your land; it shall besiege you in all your towns throughout the land that the LORD your God has given you. [53] In the desperate straits to which the enemy siege reduces you, you will eat the fruit of your womb, the flesh of your own sons and daughters whom the LORD your God has given you. [54] Even the most refined and gentle of men among you will begrudge food to his own brother, to the wife whom he embraces, and to the last of his remaining children, [55] giving to none of them any of the flesh of his children whom he is eating, because nothing else remains to him, in the desperate straits to which the enemy siege will reduce you in all your towns. [56] She who is the most refined and gentle among you, so gentle and refined that she does not venture to set the sole of her foot on the ground, will begrudge food to the husband whom she embraces, to her own son, and to her own daughter, [57] begrudging even the afterbirth that comes out from between her thighs, and the children that she bears, because she is eating them in secret for lack of anything else, in the desperate straits to which the enemy siege will reduce you in your towns.

[58] If you do not diligently observe all the words of this law that are written in this book, fearing this glorious and awesome name, the LORD your God, [59] then the LORD will overwhelm both you and your offspring with severe and lasting afflictions and grievous and lasting maladies. [60] He will bring back upon you all the diseases of Egypt, of which you were in dread, and they shall cling to you. [61] Every other malady and affliction, even though not recorded in the book of this law, the LORD will inflict on you until you are destroyed. [62] Although once you were as numerous as the stars in heaven, you shall be left few in number, because you did not obey the LORD your God. [63] And just as the LORD took delight in making you prosperous and numerous, so the LORD will take delight in bringing you to ruin and destruction; you shall be plucked off the land that you are entering to possess.

[64] The LORD will scatter you among all peoples, from one end of the earth to the other; and there you shall serve other gods, of wood and stone, which neither you nor your ancestors have known. [65] Among those nations you shall find no ease, no resting place for the sole of your foot. There the LORD will give you a trembling heart, failing eyes, and a languishing spirit. [66] Your life shall hang in doubt before you; night and day you shall be in dread, with no assurance of your life. [67] In the morning you shall say, "If only it were evening!" and at evening you shall say, "If only it were morning!"—because of the dread that your heart shall feel and the sights that your eyes shall see. [68] The LORD will bring you back in ships to Egypt, by a route that I promised you would never see again; and there you shall offer yourselves for sale to your enemies as male and female slaves, but there will be no buyer. . . .

A Note on Deuteronomy 29:1–17

Chapters 29—32 form the third major section of Deuteronomy (compare 29:1 with 1:1 and 4:44–45). This material emphasizes the covenant ratification process that demands a decision from Moses' immediate audience, the generation that did not participate directly in the covenant given at Sinai (Horeb). While the prologue to the Ten Commandments emphasized the applicability of the Horeb covenant to all future generations (5:2–3), here the text suggests that a new generation requires a new covenant. That is, each generation must in some sense *choose* to accept the Lord's offer to be their God, and for them to be the Lord's covenant people. The invocation of a new covenant is echoed in the prophetic books (see Jeremiah 30–31, especially 31:31) and, of course, helped shape the identity of the early church (Luke 22:20; 2 Cor. 3:6).

Israel, as the vassal, is described with the most inclusive terms (comprising even "aliens" and "those who are not here with us today," Deut. 29:11, 15). Again Moses calls for remembering the grand central story (vv. 2–8, 16) as the basis for the people's covenant identity as the Lord's people (v. 13). Deuteronomy 29 then concludes with additional warnings about disobedience.

Deuteronomy 29:18–29

29:18 **It may be that there is among you a man or woman, or a family or tribe, whose heart is already turning away from the LORD your God to serve the gods of those nations. It may be that there is among you a root sprouting poisonous and bitter growth. 19 All who hear the words of this oath and bless themselves, thinking in their hearts, "We are safe even though we go our own stubborn ways" (thus bringing disaster on moist and dry alike)— 20 the LORD will be unwilling to pardon them, for the LORD's anger and passion will smoke against them. All the curses written in this book will descend on them, and the LORD will blot out their names from under heaven. 21 The LORD will single them out from all the tribes of Israel for calamity, in accordance with all the curses of the covenant written in this book of the law. 22 The next generation, your children who rise up after you, as well as the foreigner who comes from a distant country, will see the devastation of that land and the afflictions with which the LORD has afflicted it— 23 all its soil burned out by sulfur and salt, nothing planted, nothing sprouting, unable to support any vegetation, like the destruction of Sodom and Gomorrah, Admah and Zeboiim, which the LORD destroyed in his fierce anger— 24 they and indeed all the nations will wonder, "Why has the LORD done thus to this land? What caused this great display of anger?" 25 They will conclude, "It is because they abandoned the covenant of the LORD, the God of their ancestors, which he made with them when he brought them out of the land of Egypt. 26 They turned and served other gods, worshiping them, gods whom they had not known and whom he had not allotted to them; 27 so the anger of the LORD was kindled against that land, bringing on it every curse written in this book. 28 The LORD uprooted them from their land in anger, fury,**

and great wrath, and cast them into another land, as is now the case." 29 The
secret things belong to the LORD our God, but he revealed things belong to
us and to our children forever, to observe all the words of this law.

Sometime around 660 B.C.E. the Assyrian king Ashurbanipal recorded
the following report in his official annals of the defeat of one of his rebellious vassals, Uate':

> Irra, my warrior god [i.e. pestilence] struck down Uate', as well as his army,
> who had not kept the oaths sworn to me and had fled before the onslaught
> of Ashur, my god. . . . Famine broke out among them and they ate the flesh
> of their children against their hunger. My gods inflicted quickly upon them
> all the curses written in their sworn agreements. Even when their animals
> suckled many times, they could not fill their stomachs with milk. Whenever
> the inhabitants of Arabia asked each other, 'On account of what have these
> calamities befallen Arabia?' [they answered themselves:] 'Because we did
> not keep the solemn oaths sworn by Ashur, because we offended the friend-
> liness of Ashurbanipal, the king, beloved by Ellil! (Adapted from Pritchard,
> *Texts*, 1969, 299b–300a.)

It will be helpful to keep this historical text in mind as we consider the
blessings and curses found in the book of Deuteronomy. There we can
read precise parallels in the form of dire predictions: plague affecting both
people and animals (28:18, 21–22), starvation and the cannibalism of one's
own children (28:53–57), military defeat (28:25, 48–52), and a proverbial
saying that invokes the treaty sanctions (29:22–28).

These gruesome details were not the product of some warped imagination; they were the way that suzerains routinely punished rebellious vassals, beginning at least in the mid-eighth century. They are also the way
that both Israel (the northern kingdom) and Judah (the southern) eventually met their end (see 2 Kings 6:24–30; 17:1–41; 25:1–30). World War I
gave us the German term *realpolitik*, meaning the political realities of history, the way things really are. Ashurbanipal's report suggests the realpolitik of treaty curses.

As we have seen repeatedly, ancient Israel understood its relationship
to the Lord in terms of the political model of a treaty. In the ancient Near
East, the model normally included blessings and curses. They provided
the concrete rewards and punishments that theoretically ensured obedience to the particular regulations. We have also seen that the sanctions
were by no means the only motivation for obedience within the Israelite
covenant understanding. Indeed, gratitude for God's previous kindnesses

and the humanitarian desire for a just society are more basic, largely because they are inherent to Israel's grand central story. But the threat of punishment and the promise of reward are also part of the warp and woof of Deuteronomic admonition, and blessings and curses are the way they are expressed. Even though both present us with difficult theological questions, we cannot dismiss them outright without eliminating a major component of the political theology of the covenant tradition.

"ACTS OF GOD"

While the blessings and curses thus reflect accurately the historical realities of ancient Near Eastern political relationships, they also presuppose a worldview that contemporary people often find unacceptable. For ancient peoples, the world of nature was inextricably linked to divine power, sometimes so closely that the two were virtually identical. What happened in nature was seen as the expression of divine pleasure or displeasure with human behavior. While Israel certainly did not identify the Lord with natural forces, God was clearly in control of those forces and used them as one means of inflicting punishment or awarding favors. This worldview is closely tied to the covenant theology of blessing and curse.

Perhaps the best example of this tie is in the moral significance of rain and its counterpart, drought. There is probably no part of nature on which humans depend more than rain, especially in a geographic setting such as ancient Israel's that had no reliable water for irrigation (in contrast to Egypt). Numerous passages in Deuteronomy show that the provision of rain is a sign of God's blessing, while the withholding of rain is a sign of God's curse (11:10–17; 28:12a, 23–24; see 7:13; 8:7). The same understanding of rain is evident elsewhere in the Old Testament, for example, in 1 Kings 8:35–36; 17:1–18: 46; and Isaiah 5:6. As in the formal curses in Deuteronomy, the book of Amos mentions the lack of rain along with other natural disasters as divine punishment (Amos 4:6–10, 4:6, hunger, vegetation diseases, pestilence).

Now most of us do not understand rain this way. Perhaps in cases of severe drought, we might attend a prayer service for rain, but most of us would not consider drought as a direct divine punishment for human wrongdoing. We would also not think of human illnesses, plant or crop diseases, insect infestations (Amos 7:1–3), or earthquakes (Num. 16:29–34) as expressions of a divine curse. Insurance policies may refer to some of these as "acts of God," but most of us do not take that phrase literally.

Indeed, to make a direct moral connection between natural disasters and human suffering would almost be theologically cruel as well as care-less. Imagine telling people whose children are dying of a cholera epi-demic that they are being punished by God. Similarly, people who are killed in earthquakes may be guilty of choosing to live in a dangerous place—over the San Andreas fault, perhaps—but to accuse them of im-morality and to suggest that God shook the earth in order to execute them would be obscene. It would be equally wrong to make a direct moral con-nection between natural bounty and divine blessing, that is, to conclude that ample rain and the resultant bountiful harvest are the result of divine favor, and thus signs of perfection in the people who benefit from them.

"MOIST AND DRY ALIKE"

Another word of caution concerns the communal perspective of the bless-ings and curses. By and large, Deuteronomy presents these phenomena as social rather than personal, national rather than individual. This corpo-rate orientation is, again, inherent to the political model. The rewards and punishments of the covenant affect the people as a whole, and are thus signs of the people's obedience or disobedience.

Two exceptions will prove the rule. In 29:18–21 Moses suggests the possibility of limited retribution. God will "single out" and punish "a man or woman, or a family or tribe" who is disobedient. Similarly, in 7:10, Moses says that God "repays in their own person those who reject him." But the surrounding material in both cases is, like the rest of Deuteron-omy, addressed to the people as a whole (see 7:6, 14). Moreover, the sub-sequent text in chapter 29 clearly has a devastation in mind that is far be-yond even a tribe, encompassing the entire land and ultimately involving deportation of the population to another country (exile; vv. 22–28). Even in the exception, the warning appears that individual sins will bring "di-saster on moist and dry alike" (v. 19).

In both these exceptions we see a struggle to formulate a theology that does justice both to individual responsibility and to corporate guilt. That is not easy to do! The problem has appeared already in the Ten Com-mandments, where God is described as "punishing children for the iniq-uity of parents, to the third and fourth generation of those who reject me" (5:9; see Exod. 34:6–7). Elemental notions of fairness recoil at this thought. Indeed, legislation in Deuteronomy 24:17 forbids punishment of this sort, at least as executed by other human beings. The historical expe-rience of the exile also prompted extensive discussion of the problem (see

Ezek. 18). Nevertheless, ordinary experience also amply shows that people *do* suffer as a result of irresponsible parenting, often affecting several generations (many American plays are expositions, albeit secular, of Deut. 5:9—*Long Day's Journey into Night*, Eugene O'Neill; *The Glass Menagerie*, Tennessee Williams; *Lost in Yonkers*, Neil Simon). And political experience demonstrates that people are often victims of national and even international policies that they had nothing to do with personally. While we may not want to attribute such suffering to direct divine causation (any more than we do with rain), we would be naïve to ignore the intergenerational matrix of such suffering.

It is important to emphasize the corporate understanding of the blessings and curses as a dimension of Deuteronomy's political model in order to prevent the distortion of individualism. If we seek to apply the connection between suffering and disobedience, we cannot do so in individual cases, arguing that individual punishment is a result of individual sin. The covenant sanctions do not support the deduction that, because an individual is ill, he or she must have done something wrong and is being punished by God. That such a deduction was possible is amply demonstrated by the book of Job, where Job's so-called friends make just that accusation (as in 4:7–9). Indeed, the book of Job can be understood as a refutation of a neat and tidy system of rewards and punishments that cannot adequately explain human suffering. Unwarranted connections between suffering and immorality still haunt us today. This is evident from the popularity of a wise book by Harold Kushner, a contemporary rabbi, *When Bad Things Happen to Good People*, which discusses this issue.

To summarize, blessing and curse are inherent to a political theology that is modeled on international treaties, represents a view of nature that is unscientific and "primitive," and reflects a national perspective rather than an individualistic one.

We must now ask if this section of Deuteronomy, especially chapters 27—29, has any relevance for us today.

BLESSING AND CURSE
IN AMERICA

If we posed the question about the relevance of Deuteronomy to scholars of American religious history, they would probably first say, "Are you kidding?" and then would explain that the covenant tradition as a whole has infused American ways of thinking from the beginning of our history down to the present. After all, this study of Deuteronomy began with reference to John Winthrop's sermon on board the *Arbella*, in which he applied the situation of Moses' audience on the verge of the promised land to that of his own, on the verge of a land that would soon have towns with names like "New Canaan." And Winthrop invoked the threat of punishment for covenant disobedience, as well as the promise of reward for faithfulness, concluding, as does Moses, with the words, "I call heaven and earth to witness against you today that I have set before you life and death, blessings and curses. Choose life so that you and your descendants may live" (30:19). Over three hundred years later, a presidential candidate, George McGovern, quoted these same words in his final television appeal to the American public before the election.

Neither Winthrop nor McGovern was unusual in appealing to covenant traditions, or specifically to blessing and curse, although one may argue that Winthrop in particular was more willing to entertain the possibility of curse than many who followed in the tradition. Two others who were willing were Abraham Lincoln and William Faulkner, and both point to one part of the American experience that invites comparison to curse, namely, racism. We could apply the tradition of blessing and curse to the American experience in others ways; the ecological crisis, for example, could certainly be understood in terms of a curse resulting from generations of abuse of nature. But the problem of racism began virtually with the founding of this country and continues to the present, and it also presents a cruel irony to the grand central story of Deuteronomy ("we were Pharaoh's slaves in Egypt").

In his second inaugural address, at the height of the Civil War, Lincoln referred to the institution of slavery as an "offense" against God, and quoted scripture in prophetic (and thoroughly Deuteronomic) style: "woe unto the world because of offenses" (Matt. 18:7, KJV). Lincoln held a tragic view of slavery as an institution that was allowed within "the providence of God" but that now God willed to remove. The war was the terrible means of removal, "the woe due to those by whom the offense came," and a reality of history—Lincoln argued—well attested in scripture.

William Faulkner's novel *Go Down, Moses* evokes by its title the grand central story of ancient Israel as well as the Negro spiritual by the same name. In describing the self-conscious realization of racial superiority that dawns suddenly on one of the white characters as a young boy, Faulkner says, "then one day the old curse of his fathers . . . stemmed not from courage and honor but from wrong and shame, descended to him"

(p. 111). Later in the novel, one of this white man's relatives puts it more clearly in addressing a black man:

> Don't you see? This whole land, the whole South, is cursed, and all of us who derive from it, whom it ever suckled, white and black both, lie under the curse? Granted that my people brought the curse on the land: maybe for that reason their descendants alone can—not resist it, not combat it— maybe just endure and outlast it until the curse is lifted. (p. 278)

Here, to use the Deuteronomist's phrase, both "moist and dry" suffer because of the curse caused by the sin of racism and the institution of slavery. The curse is a malignant power that extends beyond those who are originally responsible, reaching down through several generations. Once invoked, the curse cannot be avoided or expelled, only endured until it is lifted.

Lincoln and Faulkner are only two among many voices—both white and black—who have found the biblical categories of blessing and curse to be instructive in interpreting the religious significance of American history. One may immediately observe that these two speak more of curse than of blessing. Inasmuch as that is true, it points to what is perhaps the most profound implication of the tradition of curses and blessings. If, as pointed out above, we cannot apply them carelessly, it is also true that we cannot reject them outright without serious danger.

For all of the problems that the covenant sanctions present to us, they *do* reveal a remarkable honesty, an openness to self-criticism, a sense that an entire society can, in fact, be wrong, and that such wrong can have devastating results that last for generations. This is why, throughout Deuteronomy, the people are urged *not* to think of their national success as a sign of ethnic superiority (chap. 7), innate ability (chap. 8), or ethical purity (chaps. 9—10).

Perhaps ancient Israel's greater gift to us *does* lie in the notion of curse, and perhaps the lesson is this: A country that cannot imagine itself under a divine curse has no business assuming itself under a divine blessing. The blessing side of the tradition, of course, is hardly missing from the American experience. It appears in every political campaign and every 4th of July observance. The phrase "God Bless America" shows up at the end of speeches, and the song with that title is sung at many patriotic gatherings and even worship services. If someone were to suggest the alternate, namely, "God curse America," they would hardly be welcome! Indeed, the very phrase "God curse America" has a deeply heretical, unpatriotic, subversive ring to it. Yet if it is a phrase that we find impossible to entertain, then, the Deuteronomist would say, we do not really understand the implications of the great commandment or the consequences of the "great society" that fails to be great.

No one could reasonably deny that racism has functioned as a curse within American history. But there are also invocations of a blessing that are far more profound than the annual Independence Day hoopla. I think, for example, of another famous speech in American religious history, Martin Luther King Jr.'s "I Have a Dream" speech at the foot of the Lincoln Memorial. In this speech, King appealed to American experiences of independence and fairness rooted in the biblical covenant tradition. He held out a dream of reconciliation and brotherhood—indeed, a vision of a great society, in which material prosperity would be equitably distributed, in which all would enjoy "the riches of freedom and the security of justice."

In effect, King sketched what it would be like for this country to live in blessing rather than curse, what it would be like if we chose the way of life rather than the way of death (Deut. 30:19–20). Perhaps the contemporary American decision in terms of racism that is comparable to the choice between blessing and curse in Deuteronomy would be to pose whether our future will conform to the hopeful vision of King's dream or the tragic vision of Faulkner's novel.

COMING HOME, WELCOMING HOME
Deuteronomy 30:1–20

30:1 **When all these things have happened to you, the blessings and the curses that I have set before you, if you call them to mind among all the nations where the LORD your God has driven you, ² and return to the LORD your God, and you and your children obey him with all your heart and with all your soul, just as I am commanding you today, ³ then the LORD your God will restore your fortunes and have compassion on you, gathering you again from all the peoples among whom the LORD your God has scattered you. ⁴ Even if you are exiled to the ends of the world, from there the LORD your God will gather you, and from there he will bring you back. ⁵ The LORD your God will bring you into the land that your ancestors possessed, and you will possess it; he will make you more prosperous and numerous than your ancestors.**

⁶ Moreover, the LORD your God will circumcise your heart and the heart of your descendants, so that you will love the LORD your God with all your heart and your soul, in order that you may live. ⁷ The LORD your God will put all these curses on your enemies and on the adversaries who took ad-

vantage of you. [8] Then you shall again obey the LORD, observing all his commandments that I am commanding you today, [9] and the LORD your God will make you abundantly prosperous in all your undertakings, in the fruit of your body, in the fruit of your livestock, and in the fruit of your soil. For the LORD will again take delight in prospering you, just as he delighted in prospering your ancestors, [10] when you obey the LORD your God by observing his commandments and decrees that are written in this book of the law, because you turn to the LORD your God with all your heart and with all your soul.

[11] Surely, this commandment that I am commanding you today is not too hard for you, nor is it too far away. [12] It is not in heaven, that you should say, "Who will go up to heaven for us, and get it for us so that we may hear it and observe it?" [13] Neither is it beyond the sea, that you should say, "Who will cross to the other side of the sea for us, and get it for us so that we may hear it and observe it?" [14] No, the word is very near to you; it is in your mouth and in your heart for you to observe.

[15] See, I have set before you today life and prosperity, death and adversity. [16] If you obey the commandments of the LORD your God that I am commanding you today, by loving the LORD your God, walking in his ways, and observing his commandments, decrees, and ordinances, then you shall live and become numerous, and the LORD your God will bless you in the land that you are entering to possess. [17] But if your heart turns away and you do not hear, but are led astray to bow down to other gods and serve them, [18] I declare to you today that you shall perish; you shall not live long in the land that you are crossing the Jordan to enter and possess. [19] I call heaven and earth to witness against you today that I have set before you life and death, blessings and curses. Choose life so that you and your descendants may live, [20] loving the LORD your God, obeying him, and holding fast to him; for that means life to you and length of days, so that you may live in the land that the LORD swore to give to your ancestors, to Abraham, to Isaac, and to Jacob.

I have already referred several times to Moses' classic challenge in Deuteronomy 30:19: "I have set before you life and death, blessings and curses. Choose life, so that you and your descendants may live." Within the context of the opening lines of the chapter (v. 1), the challenge appears as the possibility of a restored relationship with the Lord *after* the full force of the curse has come. Almost certainly, these words were meant for the exiles in Babylon, after 587 B.C.E. It is as if Deuteronomy here addresses that situation which Faulkner had in mind when he wrote about enduring until the curse was lifted. Here in 30:1–14 we again see the tension between human irresponsibility and divine grace.

Is there any hope beyond the curse? Some of the curses are so severe that we are left to wonder. Indeed, Israel will be "destroyed" and the curses will remain among them and their descendants "as a sign and a portent *forever*" (28:45–46). In a final irony, the formal curses end with the threat that Israel will be returned to Egypt, and they will be so worthless that no one will even buy them as slaves (28:68). It is a despairing thought that it would be a good thing to be able to say "we *are* Pharaoh's slaves in Egypt"!

Yet, as we have seen before, Deuteronomy contains conflicting—sometimes contradictory—messages. We saw that in Deuteronomy 4, which reveals many similarities to chapter 30, Moses threatened that Israel would be "utterly destroyed" (4:26), only to turn around and promise that "the LORD your God is a merciful God . . . and will not destroy you" (4:31). In the Ten Commandments, the threat of divine punishment extending to four generations is softened by the promise of blessing "to the thousandth generation" (5:9–10), a qualification that is echoed in 7:9–10. God's grace is apparently greater than God's judgment, a message that appears again in the retelling of the golden calf incident (chaps. 9—10), where again "the Lord was unwilling to destroy you" (10:10).

In both Deuteronomy 4 and 9—10, hope is based in part on God's oath to the ancestors in Genesis, the promise that they would become a great nation (Gen. 4:31; 9:27). This oath was made without preconditions and without the threat of termination, unlike the covenant of Horeb. Thus it closely resembles the oath that God made with David, that his dynasty would endure forever, even when God must punish their disobedience (Psalm 89:28–37). As we have observed in the discussion of chapters 9—10, Deuteronomy appeals to this tradition of unconditional divine grace at the risk of undermining the call for obedience sanctioned by threats of divine *judgment*. The danger in this appeal is what theologian Dietrich Bonhoeffer referred to as "cheap grace," that is, grace that requires nothing of the recipient. Cheap grace ignores sin, or even appears to reward it!

Deuteronomy can hardly be accused of offering cheap grace, as anyone who has read the curses must recognize. It would be difficult to conclude from the punishments meted out that God is a permissive parent. Rather, Deuteronomy wants to affirm that God is both just and loving, and that God therefore demands responsibility but also offers a way out—not from the immediate, but from the *permanent*, results of irresponsibility. The possibility of hope is rooted not only in God's promise but also in Israel's capability to change—rooted, therefore, not only in divine nature but also in human nature. What is required for hope to be realized is a movement on the part of both sides—from Israel and from God—and that movement is expressed in one word, the word "return."

The Hebrew word that means "return" appears for both human and divine movement in Deuteronomy 30. Verses 1–2 state the condition in which hope may be realized: "if . . . you return to the Lord your God, and you and your children obey him with all your heart and with all your soul." Again we hear the Shema of 6:4–5. First comes the condition, then the result, with "return" signifying God's response: "then the Lord your God will return your return . . . and return and gather you" (30:3, my translation).

The word "return" is used in four different ways in these verses: (1) "if you return," to describe Israel's renewed orientation toward the Lord (what we also call repentance); (2) "then the Lord will return" ("restore," NRSV), to describe God's restitution of (3) "your return" ("fortunes," NRSV), what Israel hopes to receive from God; and (4) "return and gather you" ("gathering you again," NRSV), as a verbal expression for "to repeat." Moreover, verse 1 also uses the word in the expression "call to mind"(= "recall"). Hence in 30:1–10 the Hebrew word "return" is used seven times.

With the various plays on the word "return," Deuteronomy is presenting a theology of hope based on a synergy. A synergy is a combination of two things that together do something that is greater than the mere sum of the two (synergy literally means "working together"). It is as if 2 + 2 = 5. For Deuteronomy, Israel's hope beyond the curse lies in a synergy of the people's renewed trust in and obedience to God, combined with God's merciful acceptance.

If we ask which comes first, Israel's return or God's, we cannot answer the question, because it does not involve a chronological sequence. In effect, both have to happen at the same time. The people need to know that God will accept them if they return—that is the purpose of this chapter. But their return is also part of the overall movement of restoration, and without it, God's return, as it were, cannot happen. It is much like Jesus' parable of the prodigal son (Luke 15:11–32). The son returns to his father expecting only to be treated as a hired hand, but when he does go home, his father welcomes him as a son before he can even make his penitent confession.

If the emphasis falls on either side of the return here, it is on Israel's. It is significant that in Deuteronomy 30 there is no direct appeal to the oath to the ancestors, as there is in chapter 4, even though there too Israel's return appears as part of the synergy (see 4:30–31). The tension is apparent in the use of the metaphor of the circumcised heart. In 30:6 Moses says that God will circumcise their hearts, implying that God will force them to be obedient, as if creating puppets. At first sight, this is a unilateral act of God that is the opposite of an earlier use of the metaphor in 10:16, where Moses commands the people to circumcise their *own* hearts. But the emphasis on the people's willing return in the previous verses prevents our reading the text this way. Moreover, the following passage (30:11–14) recognizes emphatically that the people are not incapable of the return that is required of them, that their part is neither impossible nor superhuman, but that they "can do it" (RSV). Indeed, only if they are free moral agents can the concluding challenge be meaningful, the choice between blessing and curse, life and death (30:15–20).

Beyond the grim reality of the curse is the possibility of blessing—"showers of blessing," as an old hymn puts it. That hope can become real because God is merciful, welcoming sinners home, but only if those sinners are willing to come home. The Father waits with open arms, but the prodigal must return to be saved.

15. Testament

Deuteronomy 31:1–32:22; 34:1–12

BEQUEATHING, BINDING, AND BEARING WITNESS
Deuteronomy 31:1–32:22

31:1 When Moses had finished speaking all these words to all Israel, ² he said to them: "I am now one hundred twenty years old. I am no longer able to get about, and the LORD has told me, 'You shall not cross over this Jordan.' ³ The LORD your God himself will cross over before you. He will destroy these nations before you, and you shall dispossess them. Joshua also will cross over before you, as the LORD promised. ⁴ The LORD will do to them as he did to Sihon and Og, the kings of the Amorites, and to their land, when he destroyed them. ⁵ The LORD will give them over to you and you shall deal with them in full accord with the command that I have given to you. ⁶ Be strong and bold; have no fear or dread of them, because it is the LORD your God who goes with you; he will not fail you or forsake you."

⁷ Then Moses summoned Joshua and said to him in the sight of all Israel: "Be strong and bold, for you are the one who will go with this people into the land that the LORD has sworn to their ancestors to give them; and you will put them in possession of it. ⁸ It is the LORD who goes before you. He will be with you; he will not fail you or forsake you. Do not fear or be dismayed."

⁹ Then Moses wrote down this law, and gave it to the priests, the sons of Levi, who carried the ark of the covenant of the LORD, and to all the elders of Israel. ¹⁰ Moses commanded them: "Every seventh year, in the scheduled year of remission, during the festival of booths, ¹¹ when all Israel comes to appear before the LORD your God at the place that he will choose, you shall read this law before all Israel in their hearing. ¹² Assemble the people—men, women, and children, as well as the aliens residing in your towns—so that they may hear and learn to fear the LORD your God and to observe diligently all the words of this law, ¹³ and so that their children, who have not known it, may hear and learn to fear the LORD your God, as long as you live in the land that you are crossing over the Jordan to possess."

¹⁶ The LORD said to Moses, "Soon you will lie down with your ancestors. Then this people will begin to prostitute themselves to the foreign gods in their midst, the gods of the land into which they are going; they will forsake me, breaking my covenant that I have made with them. ¹⁷ My anger will be kindled against them in that day. I will forsake them and hide my face from them; they will become easy prey, and many terrible troubles will come upon them. In that day they will say, 'Have not these troubles come upon us because our God is not in our midst?' ¹⁸ On that day I will surely hide my face on account of all the evil they have done by turning to other gods. ¹⁹ Now therefore write this song, and teach it to the Israelites; put it in their mouths, in order that this song may be a witness for me against the Israelites. ²⁰ For when I have brought them into the land flowing with milk and honey, which I promised on oath to their ancestors, and they have eaten their fill and grown fat, they will turn to other gods and serve them, despising me and breaking my covenant. ²¹ And when many terrible troubles come upon them, this song will confront them as a witness, because it will not be lost from the mouths of their descendants. For I know what they are inclined to do even now, before I have brought them into the land that I promised them on oath." ²² That very day Moses wrote this song and taught it to the Israelites.

²³ Then the LORD commissioned Joshua son of Nun and said, "Be strong and bold, for you shall bring the Israelites into the land that I promised them; I will be with you."

²⁴ When Moses had finished writing down in a book the words of this law to the very end, ²⁵ Moses commanded the Levites who carried the ark of the covenant of the LORD, saying, ²⁶ "Take this book of the law and put it beside the ark of the covenant of the LORD your God; let it remain there as a witness against you. ²⁷ For I know well how rebellious and stubborn you are. If you already have been so rebellious toward the LORD while I am still alive among you, how much more after my death! ²⁸ Assemble to me all the elders of your tribes and your officials, so that I may recite these words in their hearing and call heaven and earth to witness against them. ²⁹ For I know that after my death you will surely act corruptly, turning aside from the way that I have commanded you. In time to come trouble will befall you, because you will do what is evil in the sight of the LORD, provoking him to anger through the work of your hands."

³⁰ Then Moses recited the words of this song, to the very end, in the hearing of the whole assembly of Israel:

32:1 Give ear, O heavens, and I will speak;
    let the earth hear the words of my mouth.
² May my teaching drop like the rain,
    my speech condense like the dew;
  like gentle rain on grass,
    like showers on new growth.

3 For I will proclaim the name of the LORD;
    ascribe greatness to our God!
4 The Rock, his work is perfect,
    and all his ways are just.
  A faithful God, without deceit,
    just and upright is he;
5 yet his degenerate children have
      dealt falsely with him,
  a perverse and crooked generation.
6 Do you thus repay the LORD,
    O foolish and senseless people?
  Is not he your father, who created you,
    who made you and established you?
7 Remember the days of old,
    consider the years long past;
  ask your father, and he will inform you;
    your elders, and they will tell you.
8 When the Most High apportioned the nations,
    when he divided humankind,
  he fixed the boundaries of the peoples
    according to the number of the gods;
9 the LORD's own portion was his people,
    Jacob his allotted share.
10 He sustained him in a desert land,
    in a howling wilderness waste;
  he shielded him, cared for him,
    guarded him as the apple of his eye.
11 As an eagle stirs up its nest,
    and hovers over its young;
  as it spreads its wings, takes them up,
    and bears them aloft on its pinions,
12 the LORD alone guided him;
    no foreign god was with him.
13 He set him atop the heights of the land,
    and fed him with produce of the field;
  he nursed him with honey from the crags,
    with oil from flinty rock;
14 curds from the herd, and milk from the flock,
    with fat of lambs and rams;
  Bashan bulls and goats, together with the choicest wheat—
    you drank fine wine from the blood of grapes.
15 Jacob ate his fill;
    Jeshurun grew fat, and kicked.
    You grew fat, bloated, and gorged!

He abandoned God who made him,
　　and scoffed at the Rock of his salvation.
^{16} They made him jealous with strange gods,
　　with abhorrent things they provoked him.
^{17} They sacrificed to demons, not God,
　　to deities they had never known,
　to new ones recently arrived,
　　whom your ancestors had not feared.
^{18} You were unmindful of the Rock that bore you;
　　you forgot the God who gave you birth.
^{19} The LORD saw it, and was jealous he spurned his sons and daughters.
^{20} He said: I will hide my face from them,
　　I will see what their end will be;
　for they are a perverse generation,
　　children in whom there is no faithfulness.
^{21} They made me jealous with what is no god,
　　provoked me with their idols.
　So I will make them jealous with what is no people,
　　provoke them with a foolish nation.
^{22} For a fire is kindled by my anger,
　　and burns to the depths of Sheol;
　it devours the earth and its increase,
　　and sets on fire the foundations of the mountains.

(Deuteronomy 32:23–43, the rest of the "song of Moses," combines harrowing judgments against the people of God and against their enemies, concluding with another exhortation in vv. 46–47 to use the song as a witness in the future; see below. The account of Moses' fate in 29:48–52 represents the view of a literary source known as P ["Priestly"]; see chapter 1, above, pages 33–34. On Deuteronomy 33, see immediately below.)

Deuteronomy 31—34 focuses on the death of Moses and what his departure means for Israel, both the Israel in the text and all subsequent generations who in some way identify themselves with Israel, including contemporary Christian readers. The setting is similar to that of two patriarchs, Isaac (Genesis 27) and Jacob (Genesis 48—50). As they are about to die, they assemble those who are to be the beneficiaries of their blessing and pronounce the blessing on them (compare especially Genesis 49 and Deuteronomy 33). The original subject of the blessing was close to that of a contemporary last will and testament, granting rights to the economic estate of the dying person. Already in Genesis 49, however, and clearly in Deuteronomy, the original meaning of the deathbed blessing is extended metaphorically to include the *spiritual heritage* that is handed down to future generations.

Contemporary definitions of the word "testament" point to three different actions that are helpful here to interpret Deuteronomy. A testament can be a will, bequeathing the property of one generation to another. A testament can be a covenant or contract, binding parties together. And a testament can be a testimony, bearing witness for or against someone on trial. All three of these actions—bequeathing, binding, bearing witness—are relevant to Deuteronomy.

As I suggested in the introduction, the entire book of Deuteronomy is best understood in its final form as Moses' testament, a literary form that became popular after the writing of Deuteronomy and eventually provided the name for the two major portions of scripture in the Christian canon. Now, in the closing chapters, with Moses' death imminent, we are reminded that his words are bequeathed to Israel as a replacement for himself. Moses will soon be gone, but his teaching will remain with them.

Moses hands over his leadership to Joshua, but Joshua cannot fully take Moses' place as spokesman for the Lord because only a prophet can approximate this role (18:15–22). Therefore, at the opening of the book of Joshua, God says to Joshua, "this book of the law shall not depart out of your mouth; you shall meditate on it day and night" (1:8; much like the king in Deut. 17:18–19). Moses' words spoken to his immediate audience in Deuteronomy are represented more emphatically as a *book* bequeathed to the future, a spiritual heritage that will provide the *torah*—the "guidance"—"so that you may be successful wherever you go" (Josh. 1:7). Note the frequency of references to "this book [of the law]" in Deuteronomy 29:20–21, 27; 30:10; 31:26.

In addition to recording Moses' death, the closing chapters of Deuteronomy also record the final actions belonging to the ratification of a treaty. A legal process is at work here along with the narrative process. Once the mutual agreement between God and people was recognized (Deut. 26:16–19; 29:10–15), and the blessings and curses delivered (chaps. 27—28), the treaty model would usually also contain (1) a call for the deposit of the treaty document for future consultation; and (2) an appeal to witnesses of the treaty agreement. All these actions bind the two parties of the treaty in agreement.

Accordingly, the official deposit of the covenant text is commanded by Moses in 31:9–13 and 31:24–25. For Deuteronomy the primary function of the ark is to serve as a protection for the covenant document, rather than as a symbol of God's presence in the sanctuary. Moreover, Moses orders that the covenant text be read in public every seven years, at the year of release (31:10; see 15:1–11). This way the stipulations of the covenant will be known to each generation, and the covenant will be binding on them as well (31:12–13).

The appeal to witnesses is more complicated. In the ancient Near Eastern treaties, the witnesses were the respective gods of each party. But in the covenant between the Lord and Israel, other gods obviously could not be invoked; this was one reason why making covenants with non-Israelites was problematic (7:1–4). At this point, the treaty analogy breaks down. Moses can go no further than calling on heaven and earth as witnesses (30:19; 31:28), in effect a secularization, comparable to the contemporary oath, "by heaven." Yet Deuteronomy has another way of incorporating the notion of witness itself, and that is to conceive of Moses' words, and especially the book of the torah, as an abiding testimony in Israel's midst.

A brief look at the structure of chapter 31 is in order. The author has assembled the material in a definite pattern: (Lohfink, "Bundesschluss," 1962, 50):

Moses	1–6	future—victory—divine presence
Moses	7–8	Joshua as successor
Moses	9–13	book of the law
God	14–15	*God appears and speaks*
God	16–22	future—defeat—divine abandonment
God	23	Joshua as successor
Moses	24–29	book of the law

Clearly, the sequence of the first three units is repeated in the last three, with the middle unit (vv. 14–15) standing out. Basically, what Moses says and does in verses 1–13 God confirms in verses 14–23, and then Moses reappears in the active role for the final deposit of the treaty document and mediation of God's words spoken to him in 31:16–22.

To say that verses 14–15 stand out is an understatement indeed, for this is the *only* time in the entire book of Deuteronomy that God has appeared or spoken. Elsewhere, we hear God's words only secondhand, through Moses, in the retelling of stories or in the mediating of commands. But here for the first time the *narrator* tells us that God appears and speaks. Moreover, God's appearance is expressed by the symbol of the "cloud" that is otherwise not found in Deuteronomy (see Exod. 13:21–22; 14:19–20, 24; 19:9, 16; 24:15–18, etc.).

The result of this unique appearance of God is twofold. First, it legitimates the succession of Joshua as the leader of the people. While Moses gives Joshua a "charge" (31:7–8), it is the Lord who formally "commissions" him (31:23). Thus Joshua assumes his role with a divine authorization similar to that of Moses (see Exod. 19:9). Second, the appearance of

God also legitimates the covenant-making process and Moses' words as witness. Just as such an appearance is central to the story of the *initiation* of the covenant at Horeb (Sinai), so it is appropriate here at the completion of the covenant process in Moab (compare again Exod. 19:9, 16; 24: 15–18 and Deut. 4:11; 5:22). But God's words here also describe Moses' words as a witness. The reference is to the "song of Moses" in Deuteronomy 32 (see 31:19, 21). The word "witness" is then picked up in Moses' concluding speech in 31:24–29 and applied to the book of the law in its entirety.

The book of the law, which here most likely refers to all of Deuteronomy, is thus bequeathed to the future, binding on all generations, and bears witness to Israel. The role of a witness is to testify for or against someone on trial, and that is the role of the book of the law. Along with the appearance of God, another remarkable shift takes place in Deuteronomy 31 in that both God and Moses foretell the future. All the previous chapters hold out the future in terms of various possibilities or warnings or threats. Here, however, what will happen is stated as a fact. Perhaps the shift takes place partly to prepare for chapter 32, for God's speech in 31:16–22 seems to foreshadow Moses' "song." Indeed, the future is portrayed within the song itself in the past tense. Much of the song has to do with "growing fat" in the land and forsaking the Lord for other gods, as if chapter 8 were changed from warning ("beware lest") to indictment ("this is what you have done").

Nevertheless, the introduction of the term "witness" and the prediction of the future does not turn Deuteronomy into a kind of crystal ball. Rather, it qualifies the text as *prophecy* in the deeper sense. While the popular notion of a prophet is of someone who can foretell the future, the biblical notion is primarily of someone who can interpret the present in the light of the past (see chapter 11, above, pages 128–130). What happens in the future is determined not by fate but by faithfulness, or the lack thereof.

In this sense, Deuteronomy is thoroughly prophetic. Its role as a witness is to bear testimony throughout Israel's subsequent history either for or against the people. In almost all cases, the testimony proved to be negative—a "witness for the prosecution"—because Israel proved to be guilty. This historical judgment in retrospect is stated in Deuteronomy 31 as future. Perhaps the most graphic illustration of the function of this witness is in the good king Josiah's reaction on hearing the reading of the law: "When the king heard the words of the book of the law, he tore his clothes," a sign of mourning (2 Kings 22:10).

In designating Deuteronomy as a witness for or against future generations, the authors are already pointing toward *our* designation of this book as scripture, as "canon"—that is, as a "rule of faith." When we read it as scripture, and not simply as literature, we are implicitly accepting it as a witness to us as well. To read this book is to *be* read by it; to examine it is to *be* examined; to question it is to *be* questioned. To read it as scripture is to include ourselves within the grand central story, to say with Israel, "we were Pharaoh's slaves in Egypt" (Deut. 6:20), and we too stand beneath the mountain (5:4).

And to include ourselves within that story is to submit ourselves to the testimony of the text, to place ourselves on trial. Then we become part of the "you" whom Moses addresses, and the text speaks for us in our righteousness (for instance, 6:25; 24:13), and against us in our unrighteousness (for example, 6:10–15; 24:14–15). Deuteronomy is a testament offered to us as to ancient Israel—bequeathing to us a rich spiritual heritage, binding us to God and neighbor, and bearing witness to us in our attempt to live the word.

THE END AND THE BEGINNING
Deuteronomy 34:1–12

34:1 **Then Moses went up from the plains of Moab to Mount Nebo, to the top of Pisgah, which is opposite Jericho, and the LORD showed him the whole land: Gilead as far as Dan, 2 all Naphtali, the land of Ephraim and Manasseh, all the land of Judah as far as the Western Sea, 3 the Negeb, and the Plain—that is, the valley of Jericho, the city of palm trees—as far as Zoar. 4 The LORD said to him, "This is the land of which I swore to Abraham, to Isaac, and to Jacob, saying, 'I will give it to your descendants'; I have let you see it with your eyes, but you shall not cross over there." 5 Then Moses, the servant of the LORD, died there in the land of Moab, at the LORD's command. 6 He was buried in a valley in the land of Moab, opposite Beth-peor, but no one knows his burial place to this day. 7 Moses was one hundred twenty years old when he died; his sight was unimpaired and his vigor had not abated. 8 The Israelites wept for Moses in the plains of Moab thirty days; then the period of mourning for Moses was ended.**

9 Joshua son of Nun was full of the spirit of wisdom, because Moses had laid his hands on him; and the Israelites obeyed him, doing as the LORD had commanded Moses.

10 Never since has there arisen a prophet in Israel like Moses, whom the LORD knew face to face. 11 He was unequaled for all the signs and wonders that the LORD sent him to perform in the land of Egypt, against Pharaoh and all his servants and his entire land, 12 and for all the mighty deeds and all the terrifying displays of power that Moses performed in the sight of all Israel.

Chapter 34 is the end not only of the book but of the Pentateuch ("five books"), which is called "the Law" (the Torah) in both Judaism and Christianity. One of the major themes of the Pentateuch is the promise of the land of Canaan, first announced to Abraham (Gen. 12:1–3). Given this expectation, which is repeated over and over again throughout the following books, the end of Deuteronomy seems rather unsatisfying and strange. It is indeed odd that Judaism decided to conclude the first (and most important) part of the canon here and not at the end of Joshua, where Israel has finally entered the land, conquered it, and renewed the covenant with the Lord (see Joshua 24). Instead, the end comes here, with the death of Moses and with all of Israel still outside the land.

As a result, Deuteronomy suspends Moses' audience and all subsequent readers in between end and beginning. On the one hand, the book comes to a fitting end because the polity of Israel is now complete (see McBride, Polity, 1987). Israel *is* now the covenant people of the Lord (27:9). On the other hand, Israel's life as the covenant people is only just beginning, and the land of promise remains, at this moment, just that—a promise. So the polity of Israel is complete, but the plot of the grand central story is not. Israel has not "arrived." Israel has not "made it." Israel is poised for departure.

The result of this strange ending is that the outcome of the story depends ultimately on the readers, both ancient and modern. Defying our usual literary expectations, the *end* of the book is suspenseful, raising the question, Will Israel (and will we) really be the faithful covenant community? The ending is thus not "happy" in the usual sense of that term. It calls more for sober reflection than celebration, for self-examination rather than self-congratulation, for spiritual soul-searching rather than contentment. It is more like the "night before" than the "day after." It places us, along with ancient Israel, "beyond the Jordan." It puts us, with John Winthrop, on board the *Arbella*. It suspends us, along with every pilgrim, "on Jordan's stormy banks." Thus it calls us both to remember and to hope, recognizing that hope is rooted in memory, faith is grounded in thankfulness, and justice is the fruit of love.

Works Cited

Bellah, Robert, and others. *Habits of the Heart: Individualism and Commitment in American Life.* New York: Harper & Row, 1985.

Bok, Sissela. *Lying: Moral Choice in Public and Private Life.* New York: Pantheon Books, 1978.

Foster, Richard J. *Celebration of Discipline.* New York: Harper & Row, 1978.

Kaufman, Gordon. *An Essay on Theological Method.* Missoula, Montana: Scholars Press, 1975.

Kazantzakis, Nikos. *The Last Temptation of Christ.* New York: Simon & Schuster, 1960.

Kushner, Harold. *When Bad Things Happen to Good People.* New York: Schocken Books, Inc., 1981.

Lohfink, Norbert. "Der Bundesschluss im Land Moab," *Biblische Zeitschrift,* Neue Folge, 1 (1962): 32–56.

Mann, Thomas W. *The Book of the Torah.* Atlanta: John Knox Press, 1988.

McBride, S. Dean, Jr. "The Polity of the Covenant People: The Book of Deuteronomy," *Interpretation* 41 (1987): 229–44.

———, "The Yoke of the Kingdom," *Interpretation* 27 (1973): 273–306.

McConville, J. G. *Law and Theology in Deuteronomy.* Journal for the Study of the Old Testament Supplement Series No. 33. Sheffield, England: JSOT Press, 1984.

Naveh, J. "A Hebrew Letter from the Seventh Century B.C.," *Israel Exploration Journal* 10 (1960): 129–39.

Pritchard, James, ed. *Ancient Near Eastern Texts Relating to the Old Testament.* 3rd ed. Princeton, N.J.: Princeton University Press, 1969.

Tillich, Paul. *Dynamics of Faith.* New York: Harper & Row, 1957.

Wilder, Amos. *Early Christian Rhetoric: The Language of the Gospel.* Cambridge, Mass.: Harvard University Press, 1964.